PARENTAL INVOLVEMENT AND SENIOR SECONDARY STUDENTS

PARENTAL INVOLVEMENT AND SENIOR SECONDARY STUDENTS

Does School Matter?

Letha Ram Mohan

GYAN

The Publication of this book was financially supported by ICSSR and the responsibility for the facts stated, opinions expressed or conclusions reached are entirely that of the author and ICSSR accepts no responsibility for them.

ICSSR Consultant

Prof. Sudesh Mukhopadhyay, Tower 12, Flat No. 702, Valley View Estate, Gurgaon-122003, has evaluated the thesis and name should be printed at the appropriate place.

ISBN : 978-81-212-1240-3

First Published, 2014

Published by

Gyan Publishing House
23, Main Ansari Road, Darya Ganj
New Delhi-110002
Ph. : 23242060, 23261060
Fax : 011-23285914
E-mail: books@gyanbooks.com
Website : www.gyanbooks.com

Laser Typesetting : Rudra Computer Graphics, Delhi
Printed at : G. Print Process, Delhi

Cataloging in Publication Data—DK
Courtesy: D.K. Agencies (P) Ltd. <docinfo@dkagencies.com>

Letha Ram Mohan, 1959-
Parental involvement and senior secondary students : does school matter? / Letha Ram Mohan.
p. cm.
Includes bibliographical references (p.).
ISBN 9788121212403

1. Education, Secondary—Parent participation—India—Delhi. I. Title.

DDC 371.192095456 23

Contents

Foreword

While most practitioners and researchers support the policy direction of increased parent involvement, few agree about what constitutes effective involvement. Quantitative research typically operationalises parental involvement using a narrow set of indicators that focus on quantity rather than quality of different types of involvement. Despite the healthy family child relationships, in promoting education of adolescents, there is little discussion of the attitudinal aspect of parental involvement. Confusion persists regarding the activities, goals and desired outcomes of various parent involvement programmers and policies. Least is known about parent involvement than what is commonly assumed.

A multi-dimensional representation of parental involvement on the other hand would include motivational and mechanism aspect of parental involvement rather than at the participatory activities like attending P.T.A, helping in homework, reading with children, volunteering for school activities etc. Therefore, it makes it all the more important that such concerns be validated for Indian parents in typical Indian social and culture milieu.

The present book *'Parental Involvement and Senior Secondary Students. Does School matter?* Tries to give insight into those diverse facets of parental involvement. The author brings a refreshing approach to this multi-dimensional construct. Rather than actual involvement in the educational process, the parental role is discussed more in terms of providing an enabling, stimulating and enriching physical and psycho-social environment to the child.

I wish to congratulate the author for her sincere efforts to bring out the book-based on her doctoral dissertation. I heartily recommend the book to all parents, adolescents, school principals educators as well as counsellors.

Nagma Amin
Department of Educational Studies,
Jamia Milia Islamia

Preface

The importance of building a partnership in education is becoming more widely recognised which underscores the relational influences on the academic activities of children. Over the past two decades, growing evidence has also shown that parents are valuable resources for public education, one that remains largely untapped with optional outcome for students.

The present investigation puts forth a multi-dimensional representation of parental involvement including parents' perception of self-efficacy, role construction, modelling, encouragement, reinforcement, academic management, extent of time skill and resources and also involvement in school activities. This study is an attempt to give direction to the following questions like how should we conceptualise parental involvement? 2. What is the dimension of the construct? 3. Is there significant variation within and between schools in their parent's involvement? Since these factors are embedded in and are operating simultaneously in the academic activities of adolescents, the issue becomes complete. Therefore, it makes it all the more important that such concerns be validated for Indian adolescents in typical Indian social and culture milieu.

The study has immediacy in that it will aid educationists and guidance counsellors to understand fully the background variables shaping the academic activities. It is hoped that this book will prove to be beneficial for educationists, schools, parents, counsellors, policy-makers, and adolescents themselves.

This work would not have been possible without the support of many people.

Many thanks to my supervisor Professor Najma Amin, who offered me guidance and support throughout. Her insightful suggestions based on her vast experience, her penchant for perfection and sensible vision gave me the impetus to move forward.

I am indebted to Indian Council for Social Science Research for granting financial assistance for the publication and also to Prof. Sudesh Mukhopadhyay for his valuable inputs.

I sincerely thank Mr. A.K. Gupta for his timely support.

I must acknowledge Kathleen V. and Hoover Dempsey whose exhaustive research on parental involvement directly shaped my work.

Letha Ram Mohan

1

The Problem and its Significance

"The middle level students do not want parents that are always around, but take comfort in the fact that their parents are always around."

—Crosnoe (2001)

1.1 Introduction

In the history of mankind, education has formed a continuum and a basis for the development of human society. Through development of attitudes, values and capacities—both of knowledge and skill, education provides resilience to people to respond to changing situations and enables them to social development.

Every child that enters the portals of education enters with a cultural heritage with particular psychological traits bearing with him, i.e., the effect of family background and social surroundings. In fact, family may be regarded as an inexhaustible reservoir of experiences that leads to expansive personality. The family is a place where children learn to interpret reality (Way and Rosemann, 1996). Parents serve as significant interpreters for children, of information about the world and children's abilities. (Hall, Kelly; Hansen, and Gutwein1996). Of all the important and determining influences of childhood, the relationship of a child with his parents comes first. This is his very lifeline through which he establishes relation for better or for worse, with the rest of the world.

Various studies have brought out clearly the importance of parent's influence in shaping of ideals, in the choice of vocation and in the development of many interests and attitudes in the child. As the evidence indicate the impact of social environment and community in the development of children are very significant. The child's behaviour is determined by several factors mainly home environment, school and the community. Families are considered as the major influence on child's behaviour and overall development. Families have a primary responsibility for children's development and well-being. Hence, the partnership between the teachers, the family and the community is very crucial. The community working together is more valuable than its individual components working alone, (Ilbara, 1997). Within the family, parents are seen as the primary agents of socialisation, influencing the child both directly and indirectly. When the parents are involved in children's education, they may have an opportunity to express their views as part of the formal assessment process. They can also provide information about the child to help teachers understand pupils.

Over the past two decades, growing evidence has shown that parents are valuable resources for public education, one that remains largely untapped. The promotion of home school collaboration by involving parents in school or at home in their children's education has become a major concern for policy makers and educators as family and school are two significant contexts in which adolescents develop. The influence of these contexts, positive or negative, in shaping the lives of adolescents as they grow into adulthood cannot be overstated. The type and extent of support they receive from adults in these contexts, namely, teachers and parents, will determine to a large extent their confidence in academic abilities while at school, their future educational and career expectations and aspirations, and their faith in schools as an institution in helping them attain the educational and career goals. Within the framework of home school connections, many of the debates focus on parents' involvement in children's education.

Since many educationists and psychologists have drawn attention to the great complexity of the 'network of interrelated family environment variables' associated with children's academic activities, it would be worthwhile to study the role of parents in the learning process.

1.2 Parent–child Relationship

The linkage between family and adolescent academic experiences is part of a larger dynamic process unfolding over time. The life course paradigm views human development as an interplay between individual's developmental trajectories and the trajectories of significant others (Elder 1998). One of the most striking examples of this linked life principle is the *parent-child relationship*. Parents, through the choices and decisions they make for themselves and their children influence how their children grow and develop over time (Furstenberg, et.al, 1996). This view of the linked lives of parents and children offer unique insights into the most debated issue in contemporary society; the implications of parents influence in adolescents' well-being including adolescent's academic experiences.

One of the important, fateful and determining influences of children, is the relationship with his/her parents comes first. This is the very life line through which he/she establishes his relationship for better or worse with the rest of the world. A number of studies have documented that children and adolescents who enjoy emotionally close relationship with their parents report better psychological health in adulthood (Wellerstern 1985; Snary 1995). Increasing empirical evidence support the theoretical proposition that psychological well-being in adulthood has roots in the affective climate of one's family of origin. The quality of parent child relationship has been argued to have a significant impact on the competence, resilience and well-being of individuals.

Roe, an early theorist, suggested parent-child relationships influence personality orientations and development of psychological needs. Vocational interests and choices are some of the ways in which individuals try to satisfy those needs.

Buhler (1968), in her careful study of family relationships, also reported that in certain cases definitely positive attitudes were a reflection of the positive relationships existing between children and their parents and that in other cases, the negative attitudes of children just as surely reflected parent-child relationships but their emotional attitudes, in most cases differed from those of parents and sometimes were even the direct opposite.

The psycho-analytic thought has also been putting increasing importance on the potential of social pressures in the developmental process. The emphasis has been shifted from Freud's instinctual factors to environment as social determinants of behaviour. The Neo-Freudian thinkers have recognised this shift in understanding of child socialisation and indicated the implications of familial and parental antecedent variables to the study of human development. Empirical researches have strongly substantiated this view that there is no factor of greater importance in the development of personality than the family. Of necessity, the child is born into some family structure towards which adjustment be made long before demands of the extra familial environment begin to have an appreciable effort. It is the family that should provide the first medium in which the process of socialisation begins though too often it does not, a medium in which attitudes, ideals, values and sentiments of social significance are first acquired. As a member of a family, the individual is provided with countless opportunities for emotional as well as social adjustment. That the cultural milieu is a basic factor in the development of personality, is a widely accepted principle.

Studies have been directed towards determining the influence in personality of such factors as birth of parents, education, parenting style, involvement etc. (Fisher and Griggs 1994: Altman 1997). Of these several factors, it may be supposed that parent-child relationship would have an important bearing on development. The idea that personality formation can be defined in terms of two variables, i.e., home and environment—is entirely inadequate since it fails to account the existence of other independent variables like intrinsic structure including physical make up, temperament capacities and innate needs, development experience; which includes the factors of cultural and environmental determination, training including education; which is a process and not a part of environment as so often assured and, self-determination which is the capacity of person in making significant choices and decisions affecting his behaviour. These have resulted in the concentrated efforts of studying the relation between parents and children as the predominant factor in the personality development. Hence, individuals are not conceived as being passive entities, whose behaviour is simply the product of external factor, rather, it is suggested that individuals do act consciously so as to guide their behaviour towards an explicit goal.

To summarise, the handful of high quality of multivariable studies available, research shows that quality of parent-child relationships are linked to wide range of positive outcome such as—mental and emotional well-being, adjustments and social competence and decreasing of behavioural problems in adolescents.

1.3 Adolescence

Adolescence is an inherently fuzzy concept. It labels a diversity of young people and covers a lengthy developmental span. For this reason, most psychologists tend to describe adolescence in general terms as a period of transition between childhood and adulthood acknowledging that the boundaries and indeed the experiences of this part of life-cycle can be subject to considerable individual variation.

It is actually the second major phase in human development, when children develop the direction of greater self-awareness that is, awareness of their own emotional state, characteristics and potential for action and they become increasingly able to discern and interpret the emotions of other people as well. This is also a time when the individual lessens his/her emotional dependence on his parents, develops a mature set of values and responsible self-direction and vocational identity. The dominating task of adolescent years is the achievement of a sense of personal identity to know oneself, to commit oneself to carefully explored beliefs, purposes and values and to move into adulthood with a sense of responsibility for one's choices.

In the prevailing conditions of confusion and chaos in all walks of life, adolescents all over the world encounter highly turbulent situations. Adolescence is the stage when an individual undergoes changes, physically, socially, morally and above all psychologically. It is a transitional stage of 'stress and storm'. An adolescent of the modern world in addition to undergoing changes within himself/herself, faces a tough time in adjustment, catering to the demands and expectations of parents at home and teachers in the external world. Academically, intermediate level of schooling (Senior Secondary Level) is a crucial change period; as it is the stepping stone for further education, especially for professional courses which is considered as the best for a better future. A major turning point in adolescents' lives involves the career choice they make, while in high school. Frequently, it is viewed by family and community as a mere start to workplace readiness. However, this decision plays a major role in establishing youth in a career path that opens as well as closes opportunities.

A number of studies have attempted to compare—the belief, attitudes, values of parents and their children and also the extent to which parents opinion agree or conflict with that of children (Rogers 1972). The studies have shown that parents' potentially influence adolescent's identities.

Adolescence is a time for young people to define their place in the family, in peer groups, and in the larger community. At this stage of their lives, youth often struggle with the transition from childhood to adulthood. During childhood, they depended mainly on parents for economic and emotional support and direction, while as adults they are expected to achieve independence and make choices about school, work, and personal relationship that will affect every aspect of future. Adolescents find themselves moving from family-centered world to the larger community within which they begin to define their own identity. Part of this search for identity in the larger world may involve a recreation of the self that will allow them survive without day-to-day guidance of parents. This may result in young people naturally beginning to pull away from the family and spend more time at school, with friends, or at workplace. This in turn may result in resistance to parental influence in many spheres of their lives, and parental influences declining in the later years of high school when they are involved in searching different colleges for their study and applying for them. However, adolescents still mostly depend on their parents for material and financial support, and often require continued support if they enroll in postsecondary institutions.

Excessive interpersonal competitions, corrosive power of rivalry, far too many objectives, undue emphasis on marks, unjust comparisons and outright condemnation, feeling of worthlessness are only a few of the stress factors that torment our youngsters. Hence, the quality of nurturance that a child receives will profoundly influence its development, its vulnerability to frustration and anger, aggression, anxiety and hopelessness or helplessness it experiences under various conditions (Lids 1970).

1.4 Parental Influence

The influence of parents on occupational and educational attainment has been a subject of great interest for vocational and career educators and researchers alike. Parental Influence is a major determinant of adolescent development.

As is evident from a literature review done by Otto and Call (1988) researchers in such diverse fields as child development, sociology, demography and career development have long recognised that families play a major role in shaping the educational and career decisions.

Although some scholars have identified race or ethnic

background, gender, social class, academic preparation, and interactions with teachers, counselors, and peers as explanatory factors, other researchers (Cabrera and LaNasa, 2000, Hossler et al., 1999) have generally concurred that various forms of parental influence are significant predictors of students' college aspirations. Recognising parents as important definers and role models of expected educational attainment for their children, Cohen (1987) has explored the relationships between various operational forms of parental influence and students' college aspirations. Studies (Flowers et al., 2003; Kao, 2002; Kim et al., 1998; Levine and Nidiffer, 1997; Mau et al., 1995) have also reported positive relationships between parental encouragement and expectations and students' college aspirations.

Britain (1968) suggests that parents have a great impact on decisions that have implication for the future. Additionally, research suggests that positive relationships exist between students' college aspirations and the frequency of parental involvement in school activities (McGrath, Swisher, Elder, and Conger, 2002) and student-parent discussions regarding educational plans and preparation (Kao, 2002; Kao and Tienda, 1998; Perna 2000).

Cheng and Starks (2001) explains the potential impact of parental influence on students' educational aspirations in the following manner. A child conceptualises a particular socio-cultural reality through perceptions and the internalisation of information provided by (his or her significant) others through daily communication. As a result, children's perceptions of how significant others define and value educational categories shape their own educational expectations.

'Why do some parents have more positive influence on the formation and maintenance of their adolescent's college aspirations than other parents?' Scholars interested in this question have reported that various forms of parental influence are often mediated by both parent and child background characteristics. For example, it has been established that high levels of parental encouragement, expectations, and support for adolescents' educational attainment are correlated with having high socio-economic parents (Mc Connaught 1997). At the same time, a host of other negative conditions impinge on the children directly or indirectly like marital discord, mental disorder or criminality in the parents.

1.5 Parenting Style

General parenting styles and specific parenting practices continue to shape the development of adolescents. Parenting style refers to the way parents interact with children, meet their demands and care for them. They are broad patterns of child rearing practices, values and behaviours. In the day to day life, parents need to be extremely cautious about their interaction and involvement patterns with adolescents. The old authoritarian or disciplinarian parent has no place in the modern world. On the other hand, authoritative style balances clear, high expectations with emotional support and recognition of child's autonomy. Studies have associated this style with self-confidence, persistence, social competence, academic success and psychological development (Bloir 1997; Strage and Brandt 1999). Parents who are supportive of youth's education, involved in their youth's school and who have a firm but responsive parenting style have a positive influence on their achievement and educational attainment. Parenting styles are guided by how parents look at the child and what they want to make him/her.

Contemporary research on parenting styles at adolescent stage derive from Baumrind's (1971) well known studies of children and their families. Her parenting style typology is based on major parenting elements such as warmth, involvement, maturity demands and supervision. She identifies three qualitatively different patterns of parental authority—authoritarian, authoritative and permissive. On the other hand, Maccoby and Martin (1983) suggested four-fold typology that includes authoritarian, authoritative indulgent and neglectful parenting.

The home environment produced by each type of parenting has its own effects on adolescent functioning. Aspects of parental behaviour that have been linked to school success include monitoring of children's behaviour, providing help with school work and discussing school experiences and future educational plans (Amato and Ochiltree, 1986; Milne et al.,1986; Hoover-Dempsey et al.,1987; Stevenson and Baker,1987; Campbell and Mandel, 1990; Muller, 1993; Keith et al.,1993).

The style of parental monitoring has been found to have an impact on school success. Authoritarian and permissive parenting styles have been negatively associated with school performance, while an authoritative parenting style has been associated with achievement and progress (Baumrind, 1983; Hess and McDevitt 1991). When parents exercise firm control of adolescent behaviour through clear standards, but with open discussion and input, allowing decisions to student needs and desires, school performance is enhanced.

Authoritative parenting is one of the means through which parents exert impact on their youngsters' academic activities. Parental support and involvement have been found to nurture positive educational outcome.

1.6 Parental Support

Research has established the importance of family support, and parental support in particular, in predicting adolescents' educational and psychological outcome. The family has been identified as a critical force, more powerful and direct than teachers in their children's education (Eccles and Jacobs 1993, Muller 1987). Family support offers a sense of security and comfort (Trusty 1997).

Findings from Ma (2000) reveal that social influence at home (i.e., parental expectations and college plans for children) was more than those in school (i.e., peer influence and teacher expectations). In particular parental support has positive effect on their children's academic performance (Eccles and Harold, 1993). In this vein, Steinberg (1992) concluded that when parents were more involved in their children's schooling (e.g., helping with homework, helping to select courses, and keeping abreast of school's progress) children performed better academically and were more engaged in high school.

Emotional support from parents is related to higher levels of academic confidence (Went-Gross, Siperstein, Untch, and Widaman, 1997) and self-esteem (DuBois, Felner, Sherman, and Bull, 1994), greater school engagement, fewer problem behaviours (Rosenfeld, Richman, and Bowen, 1998), higher educational aspirations (Marjoribanks, 1997), and lower stress (Clark, 1991).

It is also important to understand the sources of support available to adolescents because this approach takes entire view of what students' experience. In addition, the type of support each source provides may also be vital. For example, emotional support from parents may be more important than the support from teachers, parents may provide adolescents with emotional support, by being sympathetic and understanding. At the same time, informational support from teachers may be more useful to students than getting this from parents. Adolescents may receive informational support, when teachers provide them with relevant information to help them make important decisions.

1.7 Parental Involvement

When parents become involved, children do better in school and they go to better schools. —Henderson (1987)

Studies have shown the involvement of parents and families in the schooling of children makes a significant difference. Parental involvement is a multi dimensional construct, closely analysed by educationists concerned with optimal outcome for students.

Glolnick and Siowiaczek (1994) define parent involvement as the allocation of source to child's academic endeavours. Goodson and Hess (1975) visualised and assessed the role of parents as policy makers, effective teachers and as supporting source for school centre may have a positive impact on children's achievement. Results from several studies suggest it as a complex relationship

(White, Taylor and Moss 1992; Yoon, Wighfield and Eccles 1993). In general, productive collaboration between school and families has been associated with high student achievement (Keith 1993), lower dropout rates (National centre for education statistics (1992), a decline in behaviour problems (Corner1984) and academic initiative and persistence (Holloway 1987).

Mattingly, et.al (2002) stated that though the last three decades there has been an emerging consensus that the quality of relationships between school and families play an integral role in student success, Parental involvement in children's education has been emphasised as a particularly important aspect of school-family relationship with significant implications for children's education.

The No Child Left Behind (NCLB) Act (2002) of U.S.A. provides a very specific definition of parents' involvement. It defines parents' involvement as the participation of parents in regular two way and meaningful communication involving student academic learning and other school activities. Parents, the law suggests should be full partners in child's learning and be actively involved at school (U.S. Department of Education 2004). Phrases in this definition such as regular, two ways, key role and full partners' support—the notion that parents are entitled to participate with the school in their children's education and that they should. Across a range of studies, a strong conclusion has emerged that parental involvement greatly influences children's learning and school success, and decisions that involves current status and identity needs.

After about two decades of research, the general conclusion regarding parental involvement seems that it helps three "partners", that is, the parent, the teacher and especially the child, while it harms none. As Redding (1999) points out, "there is substantial evidence that family engagement in children's learning is beneficial" (p. 149).

Several worldwide political, historical and socio-economic changes have increased the awareness concerning the relation between home and school and particularly the involvement of parents in their children's education. The stimulus for this increased interest has its roots in the education reforms, the democratisation of school, the accountability movement, the move to decentralisation and the question about the responsibility of child's education (Davies and Johnson, 1996). Consequently, educational and psychological research on the parameters and the outcome of parental involvement has become very popular.

Even though the term was established as a special title in the Psychological Abstracts of 1982; appreciable papers on parental involvement have been published on different behaviours and practices at home or a school, including parental aspirations, expectations, attitudes and beliefs. According to Brito and Waller (1994), parent involvement is a term that include different activities. It ranges from an impersonal visit to school once a year, to frequent parent-teacher consultations to active school governorship. It either to parental expectations (Hess et al., 1984) or to the ways parents help their children develop positive attitudes (Bloom, 1984) or to homework supervision (Keith et al., 1986). The focus on parental involvement has its roots in research pointing the positive correlation with children's school achievement (Englund et al., 2004). Indeed, a substantial body of literature, documents the existence of such relationship (Christenson, Rounds and Gorney 1992; Epstein, 1992; Keith et al., 1998, Kim's (2002). The findings indicate that parental involvement makes a positive contribution to children's educational achievement. Epstein (1992) argues that "students at all grade levels do better academic work and have more positive school attitudes, higher aspirations, and other positive behaviour, if they have parents who are aware, knowledgeable, encouraging and involved" (p. 1141).

According to Keith et al (1998), the effects of parental participation are long lasting and involvement builds a foundation for future success. Fan's (2001) study showed that parental involvement factors have a longitudinal effect on student's academic growth. Specifically, he found that parents' aspirations regarding children's educational attainment and communication about school activities and studies have a positive effect on children's academic growth. Similarly, Ho, et. al. (1999) report parental involvement factors of communication and parental aspiration had consistent direct effects for initial achievement status and subsequent actions. the chaotic state in the definition of construct of parental involvement makes it difficult to draw any conclusion across the various studies. It may also have contributed to the inconsistency of findings in this area. In fact, investigators refer to and describe one or some aspects or dimensions of the construct of parental involvement. Additionally, researchers use different methods to measure parental involvement (Christenson, Rounds and Gorney, 1992). This may have contributed to the inconsistent findings about the role of parents in children's learning process.

A new synthesis of research literature suggests parents' involvement in decisions and choices are based on own ideas and experience as well as on other factors growing out of environmental demands and opportunities. Three major factors account for parents' decision to become involved in the education of children.

1. Parents beliefs what is important, necessary and permissible for them to do with and on behalf of their children.
2. The extent to which they believe can exert positive influence in their children's education.
3. Parents' perception that the child and school want them be involved.

Researchers Kathleen V. Hoover, Dempsey and Howard M. Sandler (Vanderbilt University) reviewed psychological theories and research to influence parent's involvement. They defined the parental involvement as broad range of activities cited in the involvement literature including home-based activities related to children's learning. For example, reviewing the child's work and monitoring its progress, helping with home work, discussing school events and talking by phone with teachers. The researchers also looked at school-based activities such as coming to school for conferences or informal conversations, volunteering at school or serving on parent-teacher advisory board. Parental involvement in their child's education means providing an environment that helps develop a child's intellectual and creative talents, supporting homework, and communicating with the child about classroom activities. At school, parental involvement ranges from regular communication with the school to volunteering and attending conferences and other functions.

Practitioners and policy makers alike spontaneously support the importance of parental involvement in schools; however, knowing how to engage parents meaningfully for the benefit of children is less understood. School administrators and teachers face challenges related to reaching parents in positive ways, implementing strategies that result in improved student achievement, and balancing the needs of parent's vis-à-vis educators' professional autonomy.

The most promising practices involving parents seem to be those that embrace collaboration among teachers, parents, and students. Fundamental to this cooperation is a shared definition of "meaningful parental involvement".

Epstein's (2001) research offers a comprehensive parent involvement programme, and is perhaps the most frequently cited in this area of scholarship. Epstein suggested the following frame work for parental involvement, used in many scholarly researches including funded projects of US Government.

Parenting: Help families establish home environment to support children as students. This could be done by parent education and other courses or training for parents, family support programmes to assist families with health, nutrition, and other services. Also by arranging home visits at transition points to pre-school, elementary, middle, and high school.

Communicating: Design effective forms of school-to-home and home-to-school communication about school programmes and children's progress by holding conferences with every parent at least once a year, by arranging language translators to assist families as needed and providing regular schedule of useful notices, memos, phone calls, newsletters, and other communications.

Volunteering: Recruit and organise parent help and support by school and classroom volunteer programmes to help teachers, administrators, students, and other parents, allotting parent room or family center for volunteer work, meetings, and resources for families and by annual postcard survey to identify all available talents, times, and locations of volunteers.

Learning at Home: Provide information and ideas to families about how to help students at home with homework and other curriculum-related activities, decisions, and planning. This can be made possible by providing information to families on skills required for students in all subjects at each grade. Provide information on homework policies and how to monitor and discuss schoolwork at home and making provision for family participation in setting student goals (line contd.) each year and in planning for college or work.

Decision-making: Include parents in school decisions, developing parent leaders and representatives, by active Parent Teacher Associations or other parent organisations, advisory councils, or committees for parent leadership and participation, independent advocacy groups to lobby and work for school reform and improvements and also by establishing networks to link all families with parent representatives.

Collaborating with Community: Identify and integrate resources and services from the community to strengthen school programmes, family practices, and student learning and development by providing information for students and families on community health, cultural, recreational, social support, and other programmes/services. Also, information on community activities that link to learning skills and talents, including summer programmes for students.

National Standards for Parent/Family Involvement, building upon the six-types of parent involvement identified by Joyce L. Epstein, of the Center on School, Family, and Community Partnership, recommended the following as given in the Table below.

Table 1. Six-Types of Parent Involvement

1. *Communicating*—Communication between home and school is regular, two-way, and meaningful.
2. *Parenting*—Parenting skills are promoted and supported.
3. *Student Learning*—Parents play an integral role in assisting student learning.
4. *Volunteering*—Parents are welcome in the school, and their support and assistance are being sought, where required.
5. *School Decision Making and Advocacy*—Parents are full partners in the decisions that affect children and families.
6. *Collaborating with Community*—Community resources are used to strengthen schools, families, and student learning.

Comprehensive parent programmes will incorporate six keys into an action plan that is developed and implemented by an Action Team of parents, teachers, students, administration, and community members. Epstein emphasises the need for grassroots planning involving stakeholders. In her conceptualisation, parents, teachers, and community members are coined "spheres of influence"; all stakeholders are considered equal partners in student learning.

Although Epstein's typologies are considered practical and effective, other models that attempt to formalise parental involvement there are. Lunenberg and Irby (2002) summarise seven models of parent involvement alongside Epstein's school-home-community partnership model including:

1. Gordon's systems approach;
2. The Systems Development Corporation study;

3. Berger's role categories;
4. Chavkin and Williams' parent involvement role;
5. Honig's early childhood education model;
6. Jones' levels of parent involvement and
7. Language minority parents involvement approach.

Their paper further suggests developing a family partnership center, establishing parent centers or cooperatives, and creating new options for parents as potential strategies for successfully engaging parents. At the heart of parental involvement seems to be open and effective communication.

Much research is devoted to helping teachers and parents establish positive relationship. Sharing information, empowering parents, dismantling barriers to understanding and cooperation, and recognising parents' strengths, priorities, and perspectives is fundamental to building strong relationship between home and school. There are many concrete strategies for involving parents in schools discussed in the literature. Common to this corpus, however, is the need for schools to gauge the contexts in order to meet the needs of those they serve.

1.7.1 Motivational Factors

Several studies show that parental involvement generally benefits children's learning and school success but its level involvement of involvement is not the same for all parents. A number of factors influence parents' decisions and choices. There are many reasons why parents become involved in children's learning. Parents' involvement decisions and choices are based on own ideas and experiences besides factors growing out of environmental demands and opportunities.

According to Hoover-Dempsey, Bassler and Brissie (1992), parents believe those who "make a difference" are more likely to plan activities and participate in events that require their active involvement. In other words, parents' involvement in children's educational process is dependent in part on their beliefs and thoughts as parents and those concerning their role in children's learning. Parents' involvement process has been studied from the perspective of parents. The focus of study is on the process and mechanism most important to thinking, decision making and behaviours underlying those decisions to become involved in children's education. The thrust is on the major psychological constructs that appear to influence parents' fundamental reasons for becoming involved.

Hoover-Dempsey and Sandler (1995) point out that, parents made the basic decision to become involved in child's education choose such activities shaped by their perception of skills, abilities and interest as well as other demands on time and energy.

The model of parent involvement process clarifies why parents tend to become involved in education of children: what are the mechanisms used in the process and how it leads to student outcomes. Fig. 1.1 depicts the model of parental involvement.

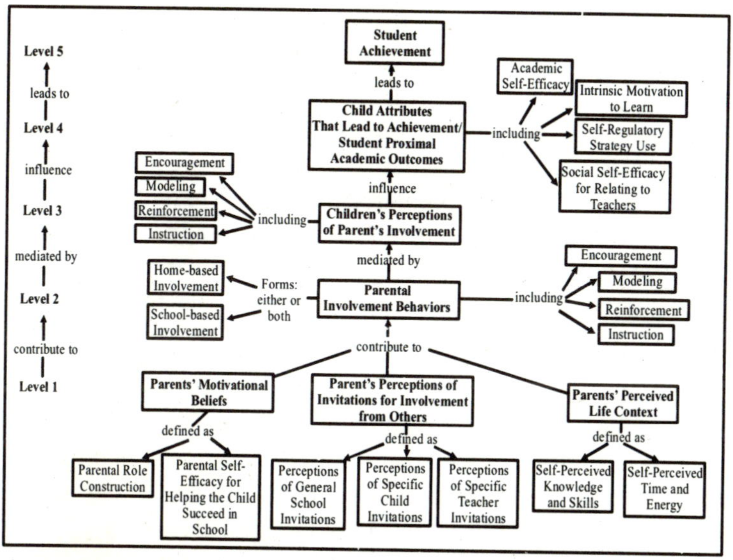

Fig. 1.1. Revised Hoover-Dempsey and Sandler Model of Parental Involvement.

Hoover-Dempsey and Sandler (1995) suggested specific variables create patterns of influence at critical points in the process. Their model includes motivational beliefs, choice of involvement forms, major mechanisms through which influences educational and related developmental outcome in children, mediating variables that enhance or diminish its influences and major outcome for child learning.

The most important construct in the decision for involvement appears to be parents' role construction. Also their sense of efficacy appears very important to the basic involvement decision. Parents' belief that she or he is indeed capable of helping the child certainly augments the power of role construction to enable a positive decision.

In brief, a stronger sense of efficacy shown by related variables seems essential to positive parental decision about involvement. This is because, the sense of efficacy for helping children succeed in school which fundamentally motivates a parent choose or (not to choose, in the case of low efficacy) an active involvement role in children's education. The predisposition is grounded in parents' beliefs that personal actions related to the child's schooling will be effective in improving schools' outcome. Rooted in the outcome about personal involvement, parents who hold a positive sense of efficacy for helping children, success in school are likely to choose involvement. This is particularly true, if the parents hold a role construction affirming the importance and appropriateness of involvement in children's schooling, and if they perceive general opportunities and demands for involvement from the child and its school.

Eccles and Harold (1993) defined parents' efficacy beliefs due to three variables, "parents' confidence that they can help children with school work; views of their competence as children progress to higher grades, and beliefs they can influence the school through school governance". Eccles and Harold suggested lower involvement or non-involvement may be due to decrease in parents' feelings of efficacy as children's work becomes more advanced.

1.7.2 Mechanisms of Involvement

The psychological mechanism which the parents engage in when they enact such activities and behaviours studied by Kahleen-Hoover Demsey. Four major mechanisms were identified in their model (Fig. 1), namely, parental encouragement, modeling, reinforcement, and instruction. Consideration of related work by Martinez-Pons (1996) had led to the development of scales to assess parents' reports on the identified mechanisms.

Parental Encouragement: This focused on parents 'explicit effective support for student's engagement in school or learning-related activities (e.g., Hess and Holloway, 1984; Steinberg, Lamborn, Dornbusch and Darling, 1992). Self-efficacy for learning and varied learning strategies.

Modelling Behaviour: Modelling theory suggests students learn in part by observing models (e.g., Bandura, 1997; Schunk, 1989). Modeling is especially effective when undertaken by adults, particularly parents, whom children perceive to be responsive, competent, powerful, and accessible (Bandura, 1997), to the extent that parents and children engage in reciprocal interactions related to school activities and their interaction involve cognitions and behaviours related to school learning, parental involvement is likely to influence student school outcomes through parental modelling.

Reinforcement: Reinforcement references the fundamental learning principle that behaviour patterns occur and are maintained because of their consequences (e.g., Skinner, 1989). Applied to student learning, reinforcement theory and related research suggests children will repeat behaviours (or learn patterns of behaviours) when they consistently associate with the behaviours receiving positive reinforcement. Of particular interest thus are parents' reinforcing behaviour that develops and maintains student attributes associate with positive learning outcome.

Instructions: Parental instruction emerges in social interactions between parent and child during involvement activities, as they engage in shared thinking related to learning strategies and processes (e.g., Goncu and Rogoff, 1998; Rogoff and Wertsch, 1984), collaborate on learning skills, tasks, strategies and outcome within the student's 'zone of proximal development' (Vygotsky, 1978), and engage in more direct instructional strategies (e.g., Sigel, 1990) that may be closed-ended (e.g., focused on memorisation) or open-ended (e.g., focused on developing conceptual understanding).

It becomes evident that parents may engage various psychological mechanism when they enact involvement activities.

1.7.3 Parental Involvement and Student Outcome

Studies show that the involvement of parents and families in the schooling of their children makes a significant difference. Regardless of income and background, students with parents involved in academic career are more likely to earn high grades and test scores, enroll in higher level programmes and get promoted. These students attend school regularly and show improved behaviour. Parental expectations and support seem to be related to children's grades.

Beyer (1995) indicates that parental academic encouragement fosters children's cognitive development. Research on long term identity goal achievement suggests the function of family in the adolescent achievement process is significant. Parental involvement plays a significant role in children's education and affects their achievement in the long run. Over the last ten years, studies have found parental involvement in education is associated with higher grades and test scores; better attendance; more homework completion; more positive attitudes and behaviours; and higher graduation and college attendance rates. When families, schools and communities work collaboratively the following specific outcome have been documented.

- Higher student achievement,
- Improved student behaviour and attendance and
- More positive school climates (Henderson and Mapp 2002).

Additional studies have found involving the entire family improves student outcome. When parents are involved at schools, their children go to better schools. The closer the family-school relationship is to a well-planned partnership, the higher the student achievement. Also parental expectation of children's educational achievement have the strongest positive relationship with the children's actual level of achievement.

While studies indicate parental involvement a important to a child's future, parent involvement in education and schools' engagement of parents remain low. Also embedded in the family climate with many parental factors operating simultaneously make this issue rather complex.

The ways in which parents involve in children's education have broadened considerably over past three decades beyond the traditional "big three"—volunteer, homework helper, and fund-raiser (Christenson and Sheridan, 2001). What parents do in the home environment, however, remains significantly more important to student outcome than what parents/families do in the school setting (Christenson and Sheridan 2001: Hickman, Greenwood, and Miller 1995: Kasprow and Fendrich, 1999; Trusty 1999). This means that parental involvement at home has significant impact on children than parent/family involvement in school activities.

Downs et al., (1981) list things that parents can offer educators:

1. ***A unique perspective:*** Since parents have been with the child all his or her life, they have a wealth of information to offer the school about the child's growth and development, behaviour, habits, feelings and responses. Parents have many insight about their children that educators never have.

2. ***The parent as teacher:*** Most of the learning that children bring with them come from parents. Even without lesson plans, teacher's guides, and formal training, many parents have successfully taught their children valuable skills.

3. ***An extended classroom:*** Even after schooling begins, much of a child's interesting and meaningful learning takes place on trips

and family outings, during talks, and as a result of other experiences offered by the parents.

4. ***A class room volunteer:*** Since the parent is the child's first teacher, the parent is naturally suited for the job of class room volunteer.

5. ***A consultant:*** Parents can be ideally consulted for any information regarding their wards.

6. ***A means for reinforcement of learning:*** The home that backs up the work of the school goes a long way to ensure good learning. Parents can provide opportunities for reinforcement of learning at home if they are aware of what is happening at school.

A growing body of literature on family involvement in middle and high school points out the potential positive influence of continued family involvement through adolescence (Catsambis, 1998; Eccles and Harold, 1996; Epstein and Lee, 1995; Hoover-Dempsey and Sandler, 1997; Simon, 2001). Because most parents regardless of race or class want their children to achieve academically and have successful careers (Catsambis, 1998; Sanders, Epstein, and Connors-Tadros, 1999), programmes aimed at informing parents about how to be involved in their adolescent child's life have increased.

It is worthwhile to explore (a) how parent involvement influences motivation and achievement of long-term identity goals, and (b) what counts as parent involvement in high school.

1.7.4 Parental Involvement in High School

Parents' involvement in their adolescent's academic life has advantages the parents' education or their gender, irrespective of the child's race or gender. Teens with involved parents, experience more success across varying situations. It is also important to note that the degree to which parents are involved also overrides the structure of the family. For example, a teen with single parent can be just as successful as s/he in two-parent home, as long as both are involved in their children's education. (Zelick)

Clearly parent involvement is important, and leads to questioning what looks like in a high school setting. Unlike the preschool to elementary years, activities such as sitting through class lesson or volunteering as an aide may not be possible or appropriate for those of older teenagers. There are other ways, however, for the parents of adolescents to remain involved. Steinberg, Lamborn, Dornbusch, and Darling (1992) suggest five ways that parents may be actively involved with high school students: namely watching teen's sporting events or other extracurricular activities, helping with homework when the child asks, aiding in course selections, knowing how their teen is doing in school and attending various school programmes.

Research suggests outside of school related involvement, regular communication with adolescents is productive. In a study of African American teens (Smith-Maddox, 2000) found that parents who had high expectation of their children, communicated regularly with children and involved in school activities were more likely to have children with higher educational aspiration than their peers.

Parental involvement in high school may take on different forms than in earlier school years, but is just as important and effective. Involvement may range from attending high school function to talking to some teen, about experiences in school. Having a parent or guardian who takes an active interest in an adolescent's progress in school and engages in regular conversation with teens, appears to be types of involvement beneficial to high school students.

Studies have validated that families have the potential to catalyse achievement orientation in their children. Well-involvement seems particularly important for adolescents from low-income communities. Adolescents face more obstacles to achievement than more privileged peers (Jencks and Mayor, 1990; Levanthal and Brooks-Gunn, 2000; Sampson, 1992). Although these adolescents have to struggle more than their privileged peers, achievement is still attainable provided their environment is supportive (Ford, 1995; Taylor, 1991; Luthar, 1991). It is not only important to think about the diverse ways in which environment can be made more supportive of lofty aspiration and achievement for adolescents but to figure out ways in which schools could partner with families to recognise and support development of additional successful strategies.

1.7. 5 School Climate

Home and school are two different entities but there is a close association between each other (Lightfoot, 1978). The school plays an important role in determining the levels of parental involvement in school. Specifically, schools can outline expectations of parents and regularly communicate with parents about what children are learning.

Research (e.g., Comer and Haynes, 1992; Epstein and Dauber, 1993) suggests a connection between the school climate and the extent to which parents and families are involved in children's education. Parents may not become involved if they do not feel that the school climate—the social and educational atmosphere of a school—is conducive, the one that makes them feel welcomed, respected, trusted, heard, and needed. When schools create a positive climate by reaching out to families to become involved, it will lead to effective partnership which in turn will benefit the children.

Schools must create a conducive climate to learning. It will be:

- Learning free of violence, intimidation, fear and threat
- Respect for educators and learners
- Free inquiry and respect for view others
- Parents and communities take up the ownership and cherish
- Innovative ideas of teaching and learning will flourish.

The Center on Families, Communities, Schools, and Children's Learning (1994) reports that parents are more likely to participate in schools, if they receive information from teachers about classroom activities, the progress of children, and how to work their children at home.

In this matter, as explained by Joyce Epstein (1995), one of the good approaches in describing the association between the school's role and parents' involvement is the partnership between the school, family and community. Epstein (1995) see parents' involvement in child's education from school's cooperation and family perspective in understanding the way school, family and community share their responsibility with students to ensure success in education. This is because, school, family or community does not necessarily contribute towards student's success; however activities resulting from school, family and community cooperation can direct and motivate student to achieve their own success (Epstein, 1995). According to Epstein (1995) the involvement of families in schools leads to overlapping spheres of influence between the home, school, and community. Thinking of the school as an extended family can help to create a positive school climate.

Schools also can provide opportunities for parents share with school personnel about parents' role in children's education through home visits, and well-planned parent-teacher conferences and open houses.

The school plays an important role in determining the levels of parental involvement in school. Specifically, schools can outline their expectations from parents and regularly communicate with parents about what children learn them. Also, schools can provide opportunities for parents to talk with school personnel about parents' role in children's education through home visits, family nights, and well-planed parent-teacher conferences and open houses. When parents talk to children about school, expect them to do well, make sure that out-of-school activities are constructive, and help them plan for college, their children perform better in school.

When schools engage families in ways that improve learning and support parent involvement at home and school, students make greater gains. When schools build partnership with families that respond to parent concerns, honour their contribution and share decision-making responsibilities, they sustain connection aimed at improving student achievement.

School climate and achievement have been correlated by several researchers (Berktold, Geis, and Kaufman, 1998; Shortt and Thayer, 1998-1999). When students feel nurtured and well assisted they fare better with educational endeavour. Furthermore, Shortt and Thayer (1998, 1999) mention "when time is used well in schools, the climate of the school improves and the opportunity for learning increases" (p. 78). In a study conducted on dropouts by the National Education Longitudinal Study of 1988, 77 per cent of dropouts reported school-related problems; of the school-related problems, 46 per cent reported not liking school, 39 per cent reported failing school, and 29 per cent reported not getting along with teachers (Berktold, Geis, and Kaufman, 1998). Students achieve lower when they sometime feel supported by teachers. It was found that when teachers and students are comfortable with each other, students adjusted better to school.

A crucial factor in establishing and maintaining forms of partnership in education of students is mutual trust between parents and teachers. Adams and Christenson (2000) found the relationships between parents and school is at higher level in elementary school than in middle or other higher school levels. As children grow older, the level of trust between family and school declines from parties involved. One of the facets identified as very important to enhance trust between parents and school is high level of home-school communication. The quality of the home-school communication seems to be better predictor of trust than the frequency of home-school contacts or demographic variables. Open communication is frequently found keyword in reports on the relationships between school and family (Hoover-Dempsey et al., 2005).

Hoover-Dempsey et al. (2005) state some evidence found for teachers and schools not very well prepared for educational partnership. School environment, climate, structure and management practices influence parents' and teachers' ideas about parental involvement and forms of partnership. In the initial and post-initial teacher training programmes, teachers could be made more aware of many aspects of parent-school relationship besides informing parents about children's learning and progress.

Inconsistencies in individual interaction between families and school personnel in various situations can undermine a positive school climate. Cultural differences bring about mixed or wrong messages affecting how families feel when they participate. Therefore, cross-checks must be made for the consistency of school's atmosphere across all types of families and situations.

While there's no doubt that school is important, a clutch of recent studies reminds us that parents are even more so. A study published by researchers at North Carolina State University, Brigham Young University and the University of California-Irvine, for example, finds that parental involvement—checking homework, attending school meetings and events, discussing school activities at home—has a more powerful influence on students' academic performance than anything about the school where the students attend. Another study published in the Review of Economics and Statistics, reports the effort put forth by parents (reading stories aloud, meeting with teachers) has a bigger impact on their children's educational achievement than the effort expended by either teachers or students. And a third study concludes schools ought to increase spending by more than $1,000 per pupil for same results gained with parental involvement.

1.7.7 Barriers

All parents, regardless of demographic background, want children do well in school (Steinberg, 1996). However, for various reasons, not all able to provide same level of support to their children to accomplish this goal. Parents who are not proficient in English, unfamiliar with schooling system, for example, find it hard to provide social and emotional support when their children face problems. Often, adolescents who experience such discontinuity between home and school seldom approach parents and family members for help with school related problems because they are aware of parents' difficulty in communicating with school personnel

(Cao, 1994). Consequently, these students may not receive the emotional support from parents that would encourage confidence in school.

Parents differ both in how they approach family-school interaction and in the skills they bring to such interactions. Many working class and minority parents lack a sense of efficacy, when dealing with teachers (Lareau, 1996). They sense a separation between home and school and turn over the task of educating children to teachers, maintaining minimal involvement with school and the children's schoolwork. Thus, parents' feelings of inefficacy can inhibit them from providing needed emotional support to their children.

Parents, regardless of level of emotional support they provide, are sometimes not well equipped to provide informational support. They differ in level of expertise to help children make informed decisions about future (Lareau, 1987). Poor minority parents, who may have high educational and professional aspirations for children, are hindered in their ability to help their adolescents achieve their goals, because they do not possess the knowledge of resources available in school (Cooper et al., 1994). Often, parents with little formal education or seldom speak English experience difficulty in understanding and intervening in their adolescents course, placements (Useem, 1991).

For some parents, particularly those who have experienced academic failure; schools are likely to evoke painful memories and deep-rooted feelings of inefficacy. Many of these are skeptical that schools can better the lives of children (Cooper, Jackson, and Lopez, 1998). This may translate into inability on the part of parents to provide adequate emotional and instrumental support to children. Adolescents socialised within such family contexts are likely to incorporate the parents' skeptical beliefs about education into their own belief system. This may have negative consequences as adolescents attempt to establish their own identity and develop a sense of their future (Eccles, Wigfield, and Grotevant, 1998). Lack of school related support, emotional and informational, from parents increases the likelihood that students may become pessimistic about the role of education for advancing socio-economic status and less likely to value educational attainment and academic achievement.

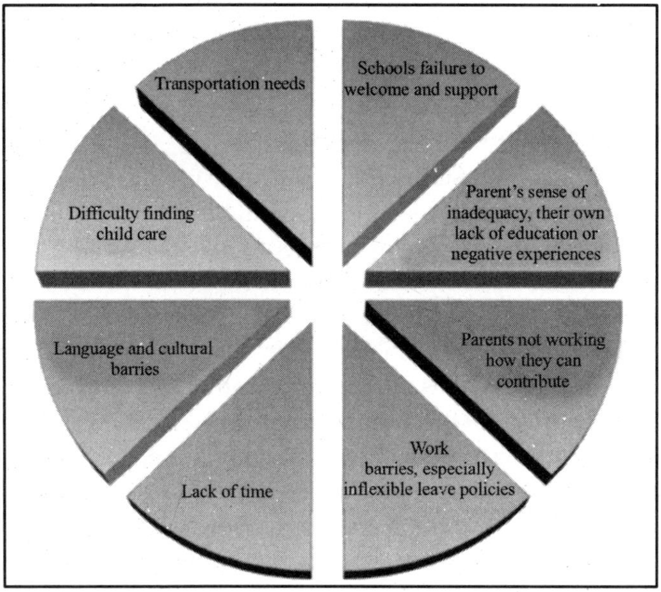

Fig. 1.2. Barriers to Parent Involvement.

Some parents are reluctant to engage in their children's education and may never perceive schools as friendly, accepting places. They may feel confused about typical school procedures and intimidated by the school staff. Others parents may believe that school provides hope for their children's future but are uncertain how to become involved. Schools must make numerous and continuous attempts to reach reluctant families through a variety of means. Some administrators, school board members, and teachers may have difficulty relinquishing their decision-making power.

Although, they may give the appearance of encouraging parent involvement, they prefer to remain in total control of making decisions. Such educators may be suspicious of parent motives for involvement. By promoting the participation of many different groups of parents and by providing numerous forums in which parents can voice their opinions, schools can prevent one person from becoming omnipotent. Fig. 1.2 shows some of the barriers to parental involvement.

These barriers can be overcome unless there is collaboration of parents, with schools, and other agencies in the communities.

1.8 Parental Socio-economic Status

Socio-economic Status (SES) is a measurement designed to approximate the relative level of economic and social privilege of a household and their access to certain economic and social resources. Socio-economic status is cited in much of the literature on youth and education as a key variable related to differences in youth outcome. In addition to using socio-economic status as an explanatory variable in analysis, it is also an important variable to use when isolating the effect of other factors on outcome. Access to resources is expected to impact a youth's life, development, and transitions as it affects access to high quality education including post-secondary education, other learning resources (people, places, and things), and availability of personal contacts in positions of influence in the labour market.

Socio-economic status is a key variable correlated to school truancy (Sharples et al., 1979; Levine 1984), school completion (Canada, 1993), the nature and extent of career exploration (Grotevant and Cooper, 1988); educational and employment aspirations (Hageman and Gladding, 1983), and occupational status attainment (Gilbert and Welke, 1997) and (Way and Rossmann, 1996). Family socio-economic status during the adolescent's formative period is seen as an important influence on post-secondary education participation, work decisions and ambition (McClelland 1990; Owens, 1992).

A socio-economic status score for a child's household is usually derived from the level of family income, the occupational category of one or both parents, and the education level of one or both parents using a standard method of ranking.

Lareau and other sociologists have described how class differences play out in terms of parental advocacy—including why poorer and less-educated parents may be less effective when they become involved.

It is important to note that there exists some evidence that children's aspirations are related to parents' educational level and occupational status (Hannah and Kahn 1989; Hill and Duncan 1987). Such findings suggest that while adolescents' aspirations and ultimate achievement patterns may be influenced positively by appropriate support and encouragement from home, the impact of such influence is constrained by fixed demographic factors such as parents' educational achievement. For example, although a child from a low-income, single parent family encouraging educational achievement may do well in school, but still aspire only to working class jobs. More recent investigations, however, have found although many family variables are important predictors of adolescents' aspirations and achievement, parents' own education is not the most important. Instead what appear to be important are issues of whether parents discuss school at home, parents' expectations for children's achievement, and parental involvement in school-related activities (Smith and Maddux, 2000).

Teachers and school administrators' perceptions of parents' socio-economic background influence how they interact with parents and whether they support or reject strategies of involvement. All too often school personnel treat poor parents from a deficit perspective, which becomes barrier for involvement. Much of the empirical focus has been on structural features of the family such as socio-economic status and parental occupation rather than process variables such as parents' socialisation practices. True, consistent finding reported in the sociological literature is that parent's level of education and occupational status are associated with children's educational and occupational aspirations. A limitation of these status attainment models is that they fail to yield explanations beyond 'SES begets

SES'. Therefore, researches have shifted focus to the exploration of family processes that may contribute to the development of adolescent's occupational identities and choices.

Several studies have found that parents' education plays a key role in shaping student's aspiration and achievement (Bayer 1995, Eccles and Harold 1993). Parents' level of education and parental support and expectations for children seems to exert some influence on adolescents' achievement motivation, (Bayer 1995). There is a positive relationship between the level of parental education and adolescents' predisposition to enter postsecondary institutions. Beyer (1995) further indicated that maternal education has positive effect on an adolescents' likelihood of seeking employment. The relationship between parents' level of education and children's achievement motivation exist because more educated parents might be more involved in children's education than less educated ones. Some research (Crockett and Bingham, 2000; Mau and Bikos 1998) suggests parent education and income influences young people's career aspirations, whereas other research (Hossler and Stage 1992; Sarigiani et al., 1990) indicates only that the parents' education is influential. Research also suggests the parents' occupation (Trice 1991) and family size (Downey, 1995; Marjoribanks, 1986; Schulenberg et al.1984) influence career-directed aspirations. In addition, the father's occupational status is highly correlated with his son's occupation (Blau, 1992; Blau and Duncan, 1967; Conroy 1997). Further, family size can be a factor in adolescent career aspirations, as larger families tend to be poorer with fewer resources translate aspirations into forms of capital, such as social capital and cultural capital.

1.9. Current Issues

Counselors and educationists accept the importance of parental involvement in schools; however, knowing how to meaningfully engage parents for the benefit of all children is less understood. School administrators and teachers face challenges related to reaching all parents in positive ways, implementing strategies that will result in improved student achievement, and balancing the needs of parents vis-à-vis educators' professional autonomy.

In a survey of 307 high school teachers in the San Francisco Bay area, more than half of the teachers reported little contact with parents (Dornbusch and Ritter, 1988). Teachers rarely initiate contact with parents; in fact Dornbusch and Ritter found 63 per cent of the teachers in their study reported initiating almost no contact with any of the parents of their students. Teachers in this study reported their job as high school teachers was complex and did not emphasise interactions with parents. Furthermore, teachers reported that when there was contact with the parents it was either to address discipline problems or to discuss a students' progress with parents that demonstrated an interest in their child's education. Thus, this report found that parents of students considered to be average with regards to conduct and academics have very little contact with the teacher. In addition, teachers in this study reported that they would not prefer an increase in the contact with such parents.

The above results are unsettling due to the fact that students of average achievement and conduct comprise a substantial proportion of every high school in our country and moreover the number of students enrolled in Government schools are very much higher than that of private schools. The results of the survey suggest that schools are not ready to embark on the road to massive change in family-school relationships.

The importance of having parents and family members support students' efforts in school is well known and well documented. Research shows a positive connection between parental involvement and student achievement. Furthermore, when schools and teachers work to involve parents, studies show that they can increase student achievement. Concern that schools may not be reaching out to families and they may not be aware of how families from different cultures perceive schools and school staff have raised questions about the effects of parental involvement for some students. Nevertheless, it appears that when schools reach out, understand the needs of families, and create parental involvement, children are more likely to experience success in school. The most promising opportunity for student achievement occurs when families, schools, and community organisations work together.

Disentangling the web of variables in the whole of family school relationship and their impact on learning is a entangled difficult task. But, it is clear that levels of engagement vary considerably depending on the parents and the context in which they find themselves.

Other research cites traditional parent involvement activities as focusing on parent participation in organised activities at school or giving parents "specific guidelines, materials, and/or training to carry out school-like activities in the home" (Lopez et al., 2001, p. 256). These limited parent involvement activities ignore cultural perspectives of minority populations. In fact, the lowest rates of parental involvement are often among minority homes (Dornbusch and Ritter, 1988). In particular, Lopez et al. conclude that this is an ineffective avenue for enlisting parent involvement in migrant-impacted schools. Matters are only made worse in that few reform efforts have made serious attempts to include families from low-income backgrounds (Lewis and Henderson, 1997). In totality, parent involvement in practice is weaker than expected. Further, when they are utilised, parent involvement activities often reach a narrow part of parent population and represent select types of parental participation.

Schools successfully engaged parents in learning, consistently reinforce the fact that 'parents matter'. They develop a two-way relationship with parents based on mutual trust, respect and commitment to improving learning outcome. Parents who are viewed as 'hard to reach' often see the school so. Where schools have made concerted efforts to engage the 'hard to reach' parents', evidence shows that the effect on pupil learning and behaviour is positive. The research shows a consistent relationship between increasing parental engagement (particularly of hard to reach parents) and improved attendance, behaviour and student achievement.

1.10 Rationale for the Study

The importance of building a partnership in education is becoming more widely recognised. A number of scholars have recently underscored the importance of relational influences on work and career factors. (Blustein 2001; Schulthesis 2003).When there is a successful coordination between community and parents; it helps children to become more competent scholars and more productive and responsible citizens. To achieve this coordination, parental involvement programmes have been initiated in the educational process so as to bring close working partnership between parents and teachers, which in turn enables to bring their unique insight, and experience to the point task of educating children and thus empowering them. When parents participate in the educational process, they enrich the academic, social and emotional development of children and help in turn parents to develop positive attitudes towards school (Kaiser 1997). Parental involvement in children's education represents rich resource for schools and communities as they seek educational success for children, and it represents a rich vein of continued parental influence in their lives, as they develop through the elementary, middle, and high school years.

The present study is intended to explore the pathways linking perceived parental values, beliefs and involvement to adolescents' academic activities. While most practitioners and researchers support the policy direction of increased parent involvement, few agree about what constitutes effective involvement. Confusion persists regarding the activities, goals and desired outcome of various parent involvement programmes and policies. Least is known about parent involvement than commonly presumed. Hence, the need to look at attitudinal components of parental involvement rather than at the participatory activities like attending P.T.A., helping in homework, reading with children, volunteering for school activities etc.

The present investigation puts forth a multidimensional representation of parental involvement, including parents' perception of self-efficacy, role construction, modelling, encouragement, reinforcement, academic management, extent of time skill and resources and involvement in school activities. This study is an attempt to give direction to the following questions like— 1. How should we conceptualise parental involvement? 2. What is the dimension of the construct? 3. Is there significant variation within and between schools in their parent's involvement?

Since these factors are embedded in and are operating simultaneously in the career aspirations of adolescents, the issue becomes complete. Therefore, it makes it all the more important that such concerns be validated for Indian adolescents in typical Indian social and culture milieu.

Despite the potential family-child relationship in promoting aspiration in adolescents, there is little discussion of what family involvement looks like in adolescents and how it can influence children's academic activities. The study is to fill the gap by clarifying motivational factors for parental involvement, the mechanisms by which parental involvement influence children's educational outcomes.

Although extensive research linking parent involvement to a variety of positive student outcome has been conducted at virtually all grade levels, educators' understanding of this link has been significantly shaped by the predominance of studies at the elementary level.

Despite the significant research that investigates parental involvement and its effects on student's achievement, the field has not produced clear and consistent results for secondary education. Differences in how researchers conceptualise parental involvement are the major reasons for inconsistent results. Some researchers conceive parental involvement as participation in school activities; others, as parental aspirations for children; and a few others, as involvement in children's learning activities at home. Only recently researchers have recognised the multi-dimensional character of parental involvement and have captured the multitude of parental activities regarding children's education.

Professionals and school personnel may not recognise that issues may inhibit parental involvement, because there is a "one size fits all" approach to describing and expecting parental involvement (Crozier 2001).

Though many researchers have discovered parental involvement, as integral to adolescent achievement, the involvement that is seen more frequently taking place in the form of talking to teens at home. There is still a majority of parents who remain uninvolved or involved very little in children's education directly.

Much of the research on the role of family in adolescents' academic activities has focused on family background but, the investigation of family processes, viewed in relationships to life roles, offers additional insight to the influence of the family.

In summary, from a research perspective, the various studies underscore the need to include both parents and children in research of this type. From a practical perspective, studies highlight the importance of perceived social support in adolescence. The technological and economic changes of the past decade, across the country, have made post secondary education increasingly necessary, and have made it more complex. Perception of opportunity, afforded by social support, clearly is important to the future planning of our youth.

Understanding the type of support high school adolescents' need from parents can make them feel academically efficacious about achieving educational aspirations. In addition, it would also give insight into whether students who have support from parents are advantageous in terms of educational outcome.

In addition, while previous research has demonstrated that there is a relationship between parent involvement and a child's academic performance, comparing outcome across these studies is difficult due to varying definitions of parent involvement and academic performance. A more thorough consideration of how parent involvement works is required.

As the research suggests, existing knowledge of parental involvement in secondary education is limited in scope. Considerable gaps in literature exist about the effects of parental involvement on educational outcome other than test scores.

About the question of parent involvement in schooling, almost everything published on this subject leaves the ideological foundation of the discussion unexamined. Either we're treated to a predictable announcement that Involvement is Good ("Parents should do more!") or else we're warned that some parents have a tendency to get well, you know, a little too involved. The message seems to be that the interest parents take in children's education is either inadequate or excessive.

Mostly studies are on the extent to which educators think parents ought to be involved. The parent's point of view is typically absent from such discussions. Also very few studies are devoted to parents' perception of their involvement. And, of course, no thought is being given to the student's perspective — what role kids might want their parents to play (or to avoid playing).

The result of the study may help in understanding the motivational and mechanism aspect of parental involvement. Recent work describing the correlates and forms of parental involvement as well as teacher and school influences on involvement has been an important part of the current effort to understand why parents choose to become involved and why their involvement often functions to create positive outcome for their children of all ages.

Given the numerous calls it seems pertinent to study the process and mechanism of parental involvement. The aim of this study is to discuss parental involvement by looking at the psychological aspect of the term (i.e., from the point of view of the individual parent). The study would attempt to understand the motivational factors of involvement and how mechanisms of parental involvement are used.

In the light of above mentioned need and significance, the investigator took up the following problem:

1.11 Statement of the Problem

Parental Involvement and Senior Secondary Students: Does School Matter ?

1.12 Objectives of the Study

The study was carried out keeping in view of the following objectives:

1. To study the motivational factors of parents to be involved in the education of their children.
2. To study the extent of the use of mechanism through which parental involvement influence children's educational outcome.
3. To study the investment of time, interest and resources by parents for being involved in the education of their children.
4. To make school-wise comparison of fathers with respect to motivational factors for being involved in the education of their children.
5. To make school-wise comparison of the fathers with respect to the use of mechanism through which parental involvement influence children's educational outcome.
6. To make school-wise comparison of fathers with respect to their investment of time, interest and resources for being involved in the education of children.
7. To make school-wise comparison of mothers with respect to motivational factors for being involved in the education of their children.
8. To make school-wise comparison of mothers with respect to the use of mechanisms through which parental involvement influence children's educational outcomes.
9. To make school-wise comparison of mothers with respect to their investment of time, interest and resources for being involved in the education of their children.
10. To find if fathers differ from mothers in their involvement in the education of their children.

2

Review of Related Literature

The review of related literature is as important as any other component of the research process. It involves the systematic identification, location and analysis of documents containing information related to research problem. The purpose of reviewing literature is to determine what has already been done that is related to one's research problem. It gives direction to the research and facilitates in interpretation of results of the study. Finally, these reviews give information which can either support or challenge the conclusion of investigator's research providing clues for later research. Studies that may be in substantial agreement or those that seem to present conflicting conclusion have helped to redefine the understanding of existing knowledge and provide a background for this research problem. Furthermore, the review not only provides suggestions made by previous investigators concerning problems in need of further investigation and hypotheses in need of testing, but it also stimulates the researcher to devise hypotheses of his/her own. Thus an indispensable prerequisite of a research project is to adequately review the relevant work which has already been done in the same area. The entire research design, can be improved by taking into consideration the research findings and conclusion of other investigations. Also a search of literature and analytical studies reveal interesting details.

If we trace the history of Parent Involvement in Post World War II (1945-1950s), it was more in the form of participation in parent conferences, homework monitoring, report card review, PTA meetings and fund raising events. In the mid-1960s educators and policy-makers in the west focused on parent involvement as a promising way to improve educational outcome for poor and under-achieving students and they developed a variety of models and strategies to promote such involvement. In the 1960s and 1970s, parent involvement mandates suggested movements for community control of education.

During 1979 and 1980 best practices and models to support involvement were developed. From 1990s till today, the focus has been on implementing strategies to promote parent, family, and community.

In this chapter, an attempt has been made to discuss relevant studies discussed under the following head—

Parental Involvement

As policymakers continue to usher in public education reform, one component is repeatedly added to the equation—parental involvement. Numerous studies have shown that parent participation in education is positively and significantly related to student achievement.

"In the last 30 years, the literature in parental involvement has grown up from a trickle to flood. Three decades of research have also demonstrated that parent/family involvement significantly contributes in a variety of ways, to improved student outcomes related to learning and school success. These findings have remained fairly consistent despite the fact that families have undergone significant changes during that time and schools "operate in very different times than those of a decade or two ago." (Drake 2000).

Britain (1968) studied the influence of parents on decision making by children and reported that parents have a great impact on decisions that have implications for the future.

In her careful study of social family relationship, Buhler (1968) reported that in certain cases definitely positive attitudes were reflection of relation existing between children and their parents.

Rajput (1982) conducted a study on the educational aspirations and academic achievement of secondary school students and effect of certain family factors. The main objectives were to examine the influence of certain family factors in the educational aspiration and academic achievement of students, to find out the effects of family environment in the educational aspiration and academic achievement of students and to examine the effect of parental involvement on the educational aspiration and academic achievement of students. The sample consisted of fifty students from class XI and XII of Gharwal schools. The main findings were that educational aspiration of students were influenced by parental involvement. Educational aspiration in families having high and medium family environment was significantly higher than low family environment. Socio-economic background had no effect on the educational aspiration of the sample.

Moles (1982) research on parent involvement provided findings regarding the effects of parent involvement on achievement and attitudes, information on the forms takes parent involvement, identified barriers to home-school collaboration and presented effective teacher practices for engaging participation. Research overwhelmingly supported parent involvement in instruction.

Dornbusch (1986) reported the results of a survey concerning the relationship between parent involvement and student achievement in six of the San Francisco Bay Area high schools. Students whose parents attended school events and engaged in contacts with teachers had higher achievement than those whose parents were minimally involved or uninvolved.

Aggarwal (1986) in her study on the effect of parental encouragement on the educational development of students (secondary stage) took a stratified random sampling of 500 boys and girls studying in class XI from twelve Higher Secondary schools of Garhwal region and divided into three groups-high, middle and low educational development. Major finding indicated that parental encouragement and educational development were positively correlated. Parental encouragement was found to have a pervasive influence on educational output of high development group regardless of gender, district and urban rural variation.

Brown (1982) Heyward and Orlansky (1984) studied the involvement of parents of handicapped children. They outlined the roles of parents as tint of advocates, resources, teachers and counselors.

The relationship among education, home support, and neighbourhood support and children's achievement was investigated by Walson, et al., (1984). Questionnaires completed by the parents of 362 first graders were analysed in relationships to children's achievement test scores. The children of parents who were actively supportive scored highest, followed by the children of passively involved parents, and then the children of non involved parents.

Various operational forms of parental influence and students' college aspiration were explored by Cohen (1987). The study reported positive relationship between parental encouragement and expectation and students' college aspiration.

Henderson (1987) reviewed 49 studies of parent involvement in children's learning at home, in the instructional programme at school, and in supporting the school in general and concluded that all forms of parent involvement have positive effects on student achievement.

Lareau's study (1987), found that middle-class parents view partnership between parents and teachers as one of the factors which affects the child's educational success at school. Apart from Lareau (1987), Reay's study (1999) found that apart from their experience dealing with the professionals, middle-class mothers bring in the habitus, which is formed by educational success into the education space.

Amritalingam (1991) conducted a study of involvement of parents of under-achievers in the Government high schools. The main objectives were to identify under-achievers, to conduct case studies for various dimensions of involvement, to develop a tool for measuring involvement, to determine the level of involvement and suggest measure for increased involvement. His finding are:

On all demographic and other critical variables, most of the parents of under-achievers did not take interest in physical and intellectual development. By and large, parents neither provided adequate facilities for studies nor did they show any interest in their wards'co-curricular activities.

Eccles and Harold (1993) in their extensive study on parental influence found parental support in particular has positive effect on children's academic performance.

While studying the longitudinal data from National Survey of Children, Wenk (1994) tried to examine the influence of mothers' and fathers' involvement during childhood and adolescence on the well-being of sons and daughters. Three independent measures of well-being, i.e., self-esteem, life satisfaction, and mental health were analysed. It was found that children's perceptions of relationship with the mother and father seem to be more salient in determining how children felt about their lives.

Henderson and Berla (1994) make an important point when they argue that there is little evidence that putting parents on advisory committees or governing bodies improves student outcome unless the parents are involved in the school and their child's learning in other ways. The best results occur when parents are involved in both learning and decision-making roles. Henderson and Berla (1994) cite several studies that indicate that schools with high achievement levels are also schools that are more open to parent and community involvement.

The study conducted by Smith (1996) was designed to measure the perceived level of parental involvement in urban elementary schools, to measure the congruency of teachers and administrators' perceptions and to investigate the relationship if any between parent involvement and student achievement. The study found that teachers and administrators have different perspectives on the success of parent involvement.

Kaiser (1997) reported that when parents participate in the educational process, they enrich the academic, social and emotional development of their children and helps parents to develop positive attitudes towards school. As the relationship and the experiences between the students, teachers, parents, administrators and other related parties develop and the schools become more meaningful learning environment, we may expect to have more effectively and productively functioning students.

Christenson and Christenson (1998); and Deslandes (1997) reported in their studies—the value of parents, families expressing confidence in adolescents and supporting autonomy as significant contributors to achievement among high school students. Their research has shown that having aspirations is associated with higher levels of mental health adjustment.

Cotton and Wikelund (2001) conducted a study on parents' involvement in children's learning and reemphasised parent involvement in children's learning was positively related to achievement. Also the more intensely parents were involved in their children's learning, the more beneficial were achievement effects. This holds true for all dimensions of parental involvement in children's learning and for all types and age of students.

Aggarwal and Kapoor (1998) conducted a study to see the influence of five best predictors of parental participation in children's academic activities on primary school students' academic achievement. The sample consisted of 42 parents of primary school children and their wards. The tool used was Mangalam Self-Report of Parents Participation in children's academic activities. They concluded that children receiving extreme autonomy in academic activities by parents are not high academic achievers. On the other hand, children not receiving autonomy in academic activities by their parents scored better. Also children receiving directions from parents were high achievers whereas children receiving neglect in their academic activities were not high achievers.

DeNeve (1999) and Diener, et al., (1999) studied the link between adjustment and aspirations. They explained that having aspirations (and therefore goals) is related to having a desire for control and it may also be an important determinant of adaptive psychological functioning since, achievement motivation, mastery over problems, general 'toughness' or 'hardiness', commitment, self-confidence, resilience, optimism and perseverance are associated with both.

Active parental involvement in young people's education tails off in terms of successful outcomes once they enter secondary school. This was reported by Crozier (1999) who suggested communicating aspiration may be more important than active involvement in the learning process because, parents may not feel they have the necessary knowledge and skills to assist, for example, with homework. This problem is likely to be particularly acute for parents who have limited educational attainments and difficult experiences at school. In addition, these parents may find formal involvement with school more stressful than those who have had better educational experiences.

Sanders and Epstein (2000) studied the nature of parent/family involvement that is most beneficial to children as they reach adolescence. Their interviews with students, teachers, and parents in four high schools revealed that although adolescents need more independence than younger children, the need for guidance and support of caring adults in the home, school, and community in their lives is very important during this time. Their model of parental involvement which is widely used consists of six steps namely parenting, communicating, learning at home, decision making and collaborating with community.

Although study habits, attitudes, and behaviour patterns may be set by a student's senior year, an adolescent's success is influenced by his or her family even through the last year of high school. This was the observation made by Kellaghan, et al., (1993); Trusty (1999) and Simon (1999).

Tizard, Schofield and Hewison's (1982) study on student achievement has shown that in children, dramatic academic progress can be realised when educators take the initiative to enhance collaboration of parents. The Haringey project in Britain illustrates just how powerful the effects of simple intervention can be in order to assess the effects of parent involvement on the teaching of reading. The researchers reported that parental involvement had a pronounced effect on the students' success in school.

Dornbusch and Darling (1992) studied the impact of parenting practices an adolescent achievement. The sample of 6,400 adolescents reflected authoritative parenting (high acceptance, supervision and psychological autonomy granting) leads to better adolescent school performance and stronger school engagement. It was concluded that parental involvement is more likely to promote adolescent school success when it occurs in the context of an authoritative home environment.

Steinberg's (1992) study focused on the dimensions of acceptance/involvement, strictness/supervision, psychology autonomy granting, parental involvement in schooling, parental encouragement to succeed, school performance and school engagement. A positive inter-correlation has been established.

After their study on parental involvement, Gramwood and Hickman (1991) have prepared a comprehensive definition of parental involvement as a process of mobilising potential of parents at home and in school for the benefit of children and their school community.

Maccoby (1990) distinguished parents along the dimensions of permissiveness and warmth. He explored the aspects of parental control stressing on sub-classifications such as consistent enforcement of demands and rules, high expectations and training, restrictive parenting, arbitrary power assertion or authoritarian parenting, open communication patterns and parental warmth and affection. He showed that supportive parenting is related to a number of child developmental outcome, e.g., self-esteem, academic success, psychological adjustment, social skills and cognitive development.

Ramiah (1990) found that there was significant relationship between parental involvement and self-concept of students. The more the parental involvement the better will be the self-concept. Female students had more parental involvement in the physical support dimension than male students. Parental involvement was relatively low in the educational and intellectual dimension.

Holdaway (1989) assessed that parents play an invaluable role in laying the foundation for children's learning and that parents cannot shirk responsibility for supporting their children's continued growth as learners. The importance of parental involvement has to be duly recognised.

In the study reported by Sui-Chu and Williams (1996), the researchers describe what parents did to support child's school progress. The researchers then analysed to what extent such activities influenced educational achievement and the degree to which parental involvement was associated with different family background in terms of ethnicity and social class. Data was drawn from the US National Educational Longitudinal Study (NELS), which was based on a sample of approximately 24,600 eighth grade students (i.e., aged approximately 14 years) in a stratified sample drawn from 1,500 schools. A great deal of evidence was collected from student and parent questionnaires completed in 1988.

Four main factors were found to describe parental involvement activity. There were two types of home involvement, one associated with discussing school activities (home discussion) and the other monitoring the child's out-of-school activities (home supervision). Then there were two types of school involvement, one describing contacts between parents and school personnel (school communication) and the other involving volunteering for school activities and attending school functions (school participation). The researchers examined the variation of four types of involvement activity across the 1,000 + schools in the sample. It was found that approximately 90 per cent of variation in involvement was within schools rather than between schools. The distribution was relatively uniform across schools. When the four parental involvement factors are taken together, it was difficult to identify schools with particularly high or low levels of parental involvement. This suggests that relatively few schools had a strong influence on the learning climate in the home or on general levels of parental involvement.

Kathleen and Hoover-Dempsy (1997)) conducted an exhaustive study on 'What Motivates Parents to Become Involved in Their Children's Education'? They found that parental involvement is linked to improved student achievement. They suggested that schools can be most effective in involving parents when they understand why parents become involved, what kinds of things they do when they're involved, and how their involvement influences several student outcome. In the four studies initially designed to investigate each 'step' in the parental involvement process, they focussed on the question – why parents get involved and examined the variables they think motivate parents to become involved in their children's education: Parents and teachers in six public schools-four elementary and two middle schools (5th and 6th grades only) participated in the study. The group included 630 parents of elementary and 259 parents of middle school students. Some general finding are: all parent variables were positively related to parents' decisions about being involved: The stronger parents' belief that they should be involved in children's education, the stronger parents' belief that their involvement will be effective, the stronger parents' perceptions what the school wants their involvement and the stronger parents' perceptions what their children need or want their involvement influence their decision.

Feinstein and Symons (1999) concluded that Parental involvement continues to have significant effects on achievement in adolescence. This conclusion is drawn from an analysis of data set from the NCDS (58) to explore the effect of parent, peer and schooling inputs on achievement at age 16. Feinstein and Symons examined the impact of certain factors (parental involvement, peer group influence, schooling inputs) on the production of 'educational goods'—in this case, achievement. The study using contemporary techniques of data analysis from large data sets have safely established that parental involvement in the form of interest in the child and manifest in the home as parent-child discussion can have a significant positive effect on children's behaviour and achievement even when the influence of background factors such as social class or family size have been factored out.

Catsambis (2001) analysed data from the NELS: 88 study and its second, follow-up (NELS: 92). This gave access to extensive data collected through questionnaire from parents, students, teachers, principals and administrators on achievement and parental involvement. Catsambis used Epstein's conception of involvement and searched the data base to assess six types of involvement, relating the measures of student achievement. Once again, background variables such as family socio-economic status and previous attainment, were factored out before examining the impact of parental involvement on student achievement, in this case in the age rage 14-18 years. The result of this study was that none of the six modes of involvement was associated with academic progression in this age range. This replicates Sacker et. al.'s (2002) finding from the UK NCDS for adolescents. However, parental involvement was positively associated with increased likelihood of making challenging course options. Higher levels of parental expectation, consistent encouragement and actions to enhance learning opportunities in the home were positively associated with students' high aspiration and college enrollment - this regardless of students / SES or ethnic background.

Cotton and Wikelund (2001) reviewed information from 41 documents and concluded — 'The research overwhelmingly demonstrates parent involvement in children's learning is positively related to achievement. The research further shows that the more intensely parents are involved in their children's learning; the more beneficial will be the achievement effect. This holds true for all types of parental involvement in children's learning and for all types and ages of students.' (p. 3)

Cotton and Wikelund (2001) note the research studies which focused on affective measures found parental involvement has positive effects on student attitudes and social behaviour. This study further notes that 'in general, active parent involvement is more beneficial than passive involvement but passive forms of involvement are better than non-involvement at all'. (p. 4)

Parental involvement has been emphasised as particularly important aspect of the school-family relation with significant implication for children's education. Mattingly et al (2002) analysed the quality of relation between family and school in relationships to student success and established positive relationships between the variables.

Additionally, research suggests positive relationship exist between students' college aspiration and the frequency of parental involvement in school activities (McGrath, Swisher, Elder and Conger, 2002) and student-parent discussions regarding educational plans and preparation (Kao, 2002; Kao and Tienda, 1998; Perna 1998).

Pienda, et al., (2002) explored the effects of parental involvement on achievement for a sample of 261 Spanish adolescents. Standardised attainment tests were used to measure achievement, psychometric tests to appraise self-concept and related personal attributes and parental involvement was rated by students. Characteristically, student aptitude accounted for significant portion of variance in academic achievement. Following that, parental involvement as rated by students themselves and taking the form of interest and encouragement, was a major causal factor of achievement. The effect of parental involvement on achievement however was not direct, rather it contributed through the shaping of adolescents' self-concept.

Sharma and Nidhi (2002) conducted study on the effect of parent involvement and aspiration towards achievement and aspiration of Class XII students. Their study explored parental factors like SES, education and self-esteem of parents and their association with achievement and aspiration of their children. The sample consisted of 310 students of classes XI and XII chosen from four schools of Chandigarh through stratified random sampling. ANOVA and Chi-Square tests were applied to analyse the data. Main finding are, (1) Parents of high and low achievement students often provided guidance to their children. (2) Academic scores of children belonging to high, average and low groups of parent involvement were not equal. (3) The academic achievement scores were different for children belonging to different parent involvement groups. High parental involvement group scored higher on educational aspiration as compared to their counterparts.

Rao (2003) made an extensive survey on relationships between parent and children. A series of formal and informal interaction with children in the age group of 12-18 years and their parents served as a critical data. The study established significant relationships between two variables. The study has also contributed significantly to analyse the problems involving psychological and social factors.

Ahuja and Sharma (2003) investigated the effect of academic achievement in relationships to parental involvement and aspiration. The sample consisted of 310 students studying in senior secondary schools in Chandigarh. A self-constructed Parent Involvement Scale was used. The results showed that high parent involvement resulted in higher achievement of Senior Secondary students.

In a study of parental support and family education on pupil achievement and adjustment Desforges and Abouchaar (2003) analysed the impact of parental and community involvement in public schools. The key finding of this report is that there are multiple ways for parents to be involved in their children's education process. Good parenting skills are essential to child's education. The more parents are involved, the higher the level of attainment of their children and *vice versa*.

The study has highlighted the important role parental involvement has on children's education. During the early years, parental involvement has significant impact on child's cognitive development, literacy and numeracy skills; such involvement is more powerful than family background, size of family and level of parental education, whereas parental involvement is related to school achievement, educational failure is associated with lack of parental interest. The most important form of involvement is what they describe as "at-home good parenting". They suggest that parenting influences operate by shaping the child's self-concept as a 'learner' and setting high aspirations.

Collinshaw et. al., (2004) highlighted the rising levels of mental health problems amongst adolescents as major concern. Apart from the involved personal distress, there are further concerns about adverse outcome. Positive involvement of parents is very much necessary.

Resmick (2005) reported that contrary to the general perception that pretty much after early adolescence, parents surrender their influence over kids and kids become beholden to peer group, parents continued to influence them.

Surabala Sahoo (2005) researched on self-esteem, educational decision-making, adjustment and academic attainment of secondary school students in relationships to parent-involvement. The main objectives were to find out the relation between Self-Esteem of students and Parent-involvement, to find out the difference between the Self-Esteem of students belonging to high Parent-Involvement group and Low Parent-Involvement Group and to find out the relation between Educational Decision-Making of students and Parent-Involvement. Descriptive survey and case Study methods were employed. Sample Study comprised five hundred students of class IX and X from five government and five public schools of North-West zone of Delhi selected from random sampling. Parents of students were taken for their involvement. Major finding of the study was positive and significant relationships between self-esteem of students and parent-involvement. Significant difference was ascertained between the self-esteem of students belonging to high parent-involvement and low parent-involvement groups. The percentage of students (53.00 per cent) having positive self-esteem belonging to high parent-involvement group was higher as compared to the percentage of students (44.44 per cent) belonging to low parent-involvement group.

Jeynes (2005) conducted a meta-analysis on Parental Involvement and Student Achievement. The result of meta-analysis indicate parental involvement associated with higher student achievement outcome. These finding emerged consistently whether the outcome measures were grades, standardised test scores, or variety of other measures, including teacher rating. This trend holds not only for parental involvement overall but for components of parental involvement examined in the meta-analysis. Moreover, the pattern holds not only for overall student population but for minority students. For the overall population on average, the achievement scores with highly involved parents was higher than those with less involved parents. This academic advantage for highly involved parents in their education averaged about 5-6 standard deviation for overall educational outcome, grades, and academic achievement. In other words, the academic achievement score distribution or range of scores for children whose parents were highly involved in education was substantially higher than that of counterparts whose parents were less involved.

In their research on the relation between parental engagement and raising achievement, Harris and Goodall (2008) explored different approaches of parental engagement and student achievement. It was concluded that parental engagement in children's learning makes the greatest difference in educational achievement.

The study by Dixon (2008) examines school level differences on different dimensions of teacher rated parent involvement and school climate while adjusting for age, gender, ethnicity and number of teaching years. Two hundred twenty-four elementary teachers from existing data and 178 teachers at the middle school level provided information on perceptions of parent involvement and school climate. Results indicate that there were no significant differences between elementary and middle school on the parent involvement scale when age, ethnicity, gender, school level, experience, were used as moderating variables. The same can be said for school climate when age, gender, ethnicity, and how certified were used as moderating variables.

Menheere and Hooge (2010) summarised in their review as worthwhile for (teachers in) schools to invest interrelationship with parents to enhance their involvement in child(ren)s' education as parental involvement matters for children's achievement, motivation and well-being at school. The involvement of illiterate parents is especially important to avoid intergenerational illiteracy.

According to PISA (2009) report, Fifteen-year-old students whose parents often read books with them during their first year of primary school show markedly higher scores in PISA 2009 than students whose parents read with them infrequently or not at all. The performance advantage among students whose parents read to them in their early school years is evident regardless of family's socio-economic background. The parents' responses show close relation between own involvement with child and child's engagement in reading-related activities during the first year of primary school and reading performance at age 15 students whose parents reported read a book with child "every day or almost every day" or "once or twice a week" during first year of primary school to have markedly higher scores in PISA 2009 than students whose parents reported to have read a book with child "never or almost never" or only "once or twice a month.

Lloyd Smith and Baron's (2010) study identifies the principals in small schools have more time and energy to support the efforts involving parents in their child's education. In contrast, the principals in bigger schools have more staff and students to be assessed; and this involves time constraints and energy. Similarly, Bartel (2010) found the school's cooperation encourages more parents to be involved in child's education at home and at school.

Vellymalay's (2012) study was designed to identify the relationships between school-parents cooperation in enhancing Indian parents' involvement in child's education. A hundred and fifty Indian students studying in National Type Tamil Schools in the district of Kerian, Perak Darul Ridzuan, Malaysia were randomly chosen on stratified random sampling. The sample comprised 50 students from Year Three, 50 students from Year Four and 50 students from Year Five. Structured interviews were conducted with the respondents. Questionnaires were used to obtain quantitative data related to school-parents partnership and the parents' involvement strategies implemented for child's education. The finding of this study indicate moderate relationship in school-parents partnership in enhancing Indian parents' involvement in child's education. The more the parents feel welcome at school, the higher their involvement in child's education. The parents also show higher involvement when the school is cooperative in discussing their child. In addition, findings also indicate that parents are more involved in child's education when the parents are kept informed about the meetings, activities and events they have to attend.

Hasumi, et.al., (2012) examined the association between parental involvement and mental well-being among 6721 school-going adolescents aged 13 to 15 years who participated in India's nationally-representative Global School-based Student Health Survey (GSHS) in 2007. Parental involvement (homework checking, parental understanding of their children's problems, and parental knowledge of children's free-time activities) was reported by students to decrease with age, while poor mental health (loneliness, insomnia due to anxiety, and sadness and hopelessness) increased with age. Age adjusted logistic regression models showed that high levels of reported parental involvement were associated with decreased likelihood of poor mental health.

While the above studies have proved that parents have a high dependency on their child's school, a child's educational attainment does not always increase with the presence and the involvement indicated by parents solely at school (Allen, 2008). At the same time, the dependency between parents and the school should not only be observed as the relationships between parents and the school. It also must be observed as the relationships between school and the parents. This is an important issue that needs to be highlighted because parental involvement at school, as proven by the above studies, is definitely impossible without direct involvement from the school.

The above studies have found that students with involved parents, "no matter what their income or background," were more likely to succeed in school-attending school regularly, earning higher grades, passing their classes, and graduating and going on to post-secondary education. The research has also suggested that teachers who hold stronger beliefs in their own effectiveness and more positive perceptions of school support for parental involvement do more to involve parents.

The importance of the family with connection to child's social and cognitive development has been highlighted in the reviews. All such familial variables that can affect child outcome, for example parental dispositions, marital and sibling influences and the socio-cultural context in which the family operates are considered within the interaction between the parent and the child. The parent-child interaction is characterised by two major parenting dimension: nurturance (warmth and support) and control (supervision and discipline).

Parental involvement is seen to have significant effect on children's achievement and adjustment even after other factors, such as social class, maternal education and poverty have been taken into consideration. Differences in parental involvement have bigger impact on achievement than differences associated with the school in primary age range. The above studies show parental involvement continues to have significant effect through the age.

3

Design of the Study

"The function of a research design is to organise the procedures of study so that error is minimised, effort is economised and relevant evidence is gathered efficiently".

— CLastrucci

An appropriate research design is a framework or blueprint for conducting the research project. It is used to structure the research, to show how the major parts of research project - namely the aims and objectives, samples or groups, measurement of variables and treatment of data work to address the central research questions. It specifies the nuts and bolts of implementing research. Research Design provides strategic framework for investigator achieve the objectives of study and obtain the answers of research questions. Furthermore, it provides guidelines for selection of the sample, construction of appropriate research tools in the light of objectives and facilitates collection, analysis and interpretation of the data. Selection of a particular design (Historical/Descriptive/Experimental/Quasi-experimental research) is based upon the purpose and nature of investigation, the types of variables to be measured and analysed and the limiting factors under which it is being conducted. The outcome of any research work based on design and methodology. Therefore, sound planning and appropriate execution of research design are the prerequisites for good investigatory task.

The present study is descriptive and exploratory in nature. Creswell (2003) suggests that exploratory studies are most advantageous when 'not much has been written about the topic or the population being studied'. The primary purpose of present research is to study parental involvement. Keeping in view of the ature and purpose of present study, the sample, measuring instruments for data collection and statistical techniques to analyse the data were decided.

This chapter describes the design of the present study. It includes the statement of the problem, description of the objectives, operational definition of key terms, hypotheses of the study, underlying assumptions, methodology, population and sample, preparation and administration of research tool, procedure of data collection and statistical treatment.

3.1 Title of the Study

Parental Involvement and senior secondary students: Does School Mater ?

3.2 Methodology

The present study is descriptive and non-experimental in nature. A descriptive study is concerned with the conditions or relationships that exist, opinions held, processes going on, effects evident, or trends developing (Best and Kahn 1993). It is marked by clear statement of problem, specific hypothesis details of tools used and procedure adopted. It involves hypothesis formulation, use of logical methods to test the hypotheses and arriving at generalisation. Often methods of randomisation are employed to estimate the error while inferring population characteristics from observation of samples (*Ibid.* pp. 120). Therefore, the present study, being concerned with existing beliefs and relationships is descriptive in nature.

3.3 Definitions of the Key Terms

Parental Involvement: It is a multidimensional term that covers the broad range of activities by parents who actively, critically, resourcefully and responsibly contribute to promoting and developing the well-being of their children. It means providing an environment that helps develop child's intellectual and creative talents.

3.4 Hypotheses

A hypothesis is a tentative explanation for an observation, phenomenon, or scientific problem that can be tested and verified by further investigation. The formulation of hypothesis prior to data collection is necessary for an unbiased investigation. One kind of research hypotheses is a null hypothesis, which relates to the statistical method of interpreting conclusion about the population characteristics inferred from variable relationships observed in the samples. It concerns a judgment as to whether apparent differences are true or relationships or whether they may result from sampling error. Based on the objectives of the study, following null hypotheses were framed.

1.1 There is no significant difference in the extent of belief of fathers of children studying in Private, Aided Central and Government schools about their self-efficacy for being involved in the education of their children.

1.2 There is no significant difference in the extent of belief of fathers of children studying in Private Aided, Central and Government schools about their roles and responsibilities for being involved in the education of their children.

1.3. There is no significant difference in the extent of belief of fathers of children studying in Private Aided, Central and Government schools about the use of mechanism of encouragement, modeling behaviours, reinforcement and instructions in the education of their children.

1.4 There is no significant difference in the extent of belief of fathers of children studying in Private, Aided, Central and Government schools about investing time, resources and interest in the education of their children.

2.1 There is no significant difference in the extent of belief of mothers of children studying in Private, Aided Central and Government schools about their Self-efficacy for being involved in the education of their children.

2.2 There is no significant difference in the extent of belief of mothers of children studying in Private Aided, Central and Government schools about their roles and responsibilities for being involved in the education of their children.

2.3 There is no significant difference in the extent of belief of mothers of children studying in Private, Aided Central and Government schools about the use of mechanism of encouragement, modeling behaviours, reinforcement and instructions in the education of their children.

2.4 There is no significant difference in the extent of belief of mothers of children studying in Private, Aided, Central and Government schools about investing time, resources and interest in the education of their children.

3.5 Methodology

3.5.1 Population and Sample of the Study

Population of the present study comprised parents of students at senior secondary level.

In India, school category is determined as per state pattern on the basis of highest class there in. A school having classes up to V will be termed as primary school, up to VIII will be termed as upper primary, up to IX and X will be termed as secondary school and that having highest classes either XI or XII will be termed as higher secondary or senior secondary school.

Depending on the management, school systems vary from Government to Government Aided, to Private to Central and are affiliated to CBSE, ICSE and State Boards.

Government School: A school which is run by the State Government is a Government or public school or undertaking by an autonomous organisation completely financed by the state Government.

Private Aided School: It is that which is run by an individual or a private organisation which receives grant from Government or local body.

Private Unaided School: A private unaided school is an organisation that does not receive any grant either Government or local body.

Central School or Kendriya Vidyalaya: All central schools or Kendriya Vidyalayas are managed by Central Government and are affiliated to Central Board of Secondary Education.

The sample for the present study comprised four hundred parents of senior secondary school students namely Class XI studying in various Private, Government, Central and Aided schools of Delhi.

To begin with, a district-wise list of existing schools was obtained from the Directorate of Education, Govt. of NCT of Delhi. From the list two Central, two Aided, two Unaided (private) and two Government schools from four districts of Delhi, namely, East, West, North and South were selected on the basis of convenient sampling technique. Care was taken to see that the schools thus selected had classes up to XII and had students studying in Science, Commerce and Arts streams. Twenty five students from each school were selected randomly. Overall, 200 students were selected. The respondents included students pursuing Science, Commerce and Humanities Stream and their respective parents (fathers and mothers).

3.5.2 Description of the Sample Groups

The sample of the study consisted of the following groups:

I. ***Students:*** 200 pupils studying in Class XI in Private, Government, Central Government and Government Aided schools of Delhi.

II. ***Parents:*** 200 fathers and 200 mothers of respective students.

Demographics of the Sample

Out of 200 students whose parents were selected, 104 were girls and 96 were boys. Sex-wise distribution of the sample is depicted in Table 3.1 and Graphical representation Fig. 3.1.

Table 3.1: Sex-wise Distribution of Sample

Sex	*Total*	*Per cent*
Boys	96	47
Girls	104	53
Total	**200**	**100**

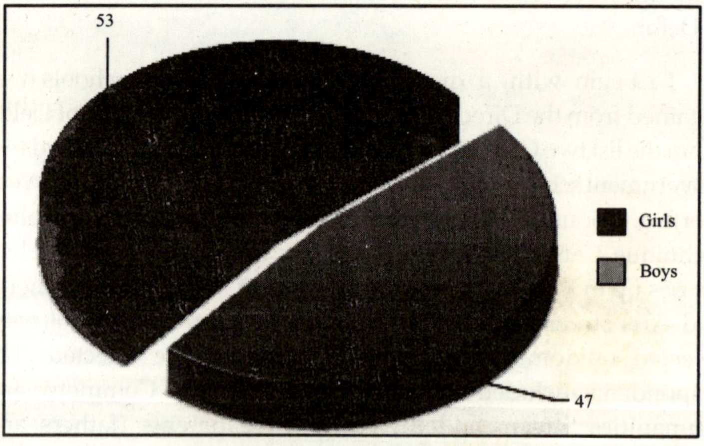

Fig. 3.1. Sex-wise distribution of Sample.

Description of the sample with reference to background variables of students and type of schools is shown in Table 3.2 and Table 3.3 respectively.

Table 3.2: School-wise Distribution of Sample

Sex	*School 1* *Private*	*School 2* *Aided*	*School 3* *Central*	*School 4* *Government*	*Total* *4*
Boys	25	19	26	26	96
Girls	25	31	24	24	104
Total	**50**	**50**	**50**	**50**	**200**

Both the parents of respective students were selected.

3.6 Development of Tools

Questionnaire for Parents: To study the perception of parental involvement, a separate questionnaire was adapted from Parent Involvement Project (PIP). Parent and teacher Questionnaire developed by Kathleen V. Hoover Dempsey, Howard M. Sandler and Joan M. I. Walker and prepared by Darlane Whetsel from the Department of Psychology-Vanderbit University. It was developed to conduct the second in a series of four OERI funded projects and was designed to examine the following questions. (a) Why do parents get involved in their child's education? (b) How does their involvement if engaged influence children's educational attainment and attitudinal variables that influence their attainment? This study examined parent involvement at various levels.

Level I: The first level focused on parent's motivations for involvement; predictors of parental involvement included parental role construction for involvement and parent's sense of efficacy for helping the child succeed the contributions of hypnotised predictors, role construction and self-efficacy that motivate involvement.

Level II: The second level focused on parents' choice of involvement forms; constructs assumed to influence these choices included parent's perceptions of skills and knowledge for involvement, parent's perceptions of time and energy available for involvement, and parent's perceptions of specific invitations to involvement from the teacher and the child.

Level III: The third level included mechanisms used by parents during involvement activities that likely account for involvement's influence on student outcome; hypothesised mechanisms were encouragement, reinforcement, modelling, and instruction.

Level IV: The fourth level focused on proximal student outcomes that lead to achievement. Parents' influence on students' school outcome may occur most directly in supporting student attributes that lead to student achievement (i.e., parental involvement's most critical influence on student learning may not be on summary measures of school achievement but on student attributes and skills that support achievement).

The questionnaire comprised many items, which were highly relevant to the present study. The reliability and validity of the tool were found to be high. Moreover, it has been used in many researches. Hence, the investigator adapted this tool with necessary modifications to suit the present study. Items related to teacher questionnaire were not included. Following were the main components of the questionnaire for parents.

(I) Self-Efficacy: Self-efficacy has been conceptualised as a set of beliefs about one's ability to perform some behaviour, task or skill, and the belief that one's behaviour will result in particular outcome (Bandura, 1986). Parental sense of efficacy includes parents' beliefs about their personal ability to make difference in the child's educational outcome through their involvement (Bandura, 1997; Hoover-Dempsey, Bassler, and Brissie, 1992; Hoover-Dempsey and Sandler, 1995, 1997; Hoover-Dempsey et al.; Walker et al). The final scale included eighteen items (e.g., "I know how to help my child do well in school). To study the level of involvement in their children's academic and career related aspects, Self-efficacy is an important indicator.

(II) Role Construction: Role Construction is about how parents perceive their roles and responsibilities in helping their wards in academic and career related activities. It includes parents' belief, values, goals and expectations related to their children's development and education, parents' ideas about their responsibilities in day today education and ideas about their responsibilities related to major decisions in the course of their child's education.

(III) Encouragement: Parental encouragement focused on parents' explicit affective support for the student's engagement in school or learning-related activities (e.g., Hess and Holloway, 1984; Steinberg, Lamborn, Dornbusch and Darling, 1992). Adapted from Martinez-Pons (1996), the scale included 14 items focused on parental support and encouragement for student's interest in school and learning, self-efficacy for learning, and varied learning strategies (e.g., We encourage this child when he or she has trouble doing school work;" "We encourage this child to ask other people for help when a problem is hard to solve").

(IV) Modelling: Modelling theory suggests that students learn in part by observing models (e.g., Bandura, 1997; Schunk, 1989). Modelling is especially effective when undertaken by adults, particularly parents, whom children perceive to be responsive, competent, powerful, and accessible (Bandura, 1997). To the extent that parents and children engage in reciprocal interaction related to school activities-and their interaction involve cognitions and behaviours related to school learning-parental involvement likely to influence student school outcome through parental modeling.

The scale was adapted from Martinez-Pons' (1996) measure, and include items developed to assess parental modeling as keyed to the student learning attributes. The modeling scale included 9 items (e.g., "We show this child we know how to solve problems."

(V) Reinforcement: Reinforcement references the fundamental learning principle that behaviour patterns occur and are maintained because of their consequences (e.g., Skinner, 1989). Applied to student learning, reinforcement theory and related research suggests that children will repeat behaviour (or learn patterns of behaviours) when they consistently associate with the behaviour receiving positive reinforcement. Of particular interest thus are parents' reinforcing behaviours that act to develop and maintain student attributes associated with positive learning outcome. The scale to assess parental reinforcement during involvement was adapted from Martinez-Pons' (1996) measure, and included items designed to assess reinforcement as related to the student learning attributes. The scale included 13 items (e.g., "We show this child we like it when he or she organises his or her schoolwork."

(VI) Instruction: Parental instruction emerges in social interaction between parent and child during involvement activities as they engage in shared thinking related to learning strategies and processes, collaborate on learning skills, tasks, strategies and outcomes within the student's zone of proximal development' (Vygotsky, 1978), The scale, adapted from Martinez-Pons (1996) measure, included 15 items (e.g., "We teach this child how to check homework as he or she goes along;" "We teach this child to ask questions when he or she doesn't understand something)."

(VII) Investment of Time, Interest and Resources: One of the most essential ingredients in involvement activities is the Investment of time, interest and resource by parents in matters of education and career plans of their children. Dialogic activities, like daily conversation with the child about everyday school events, going for outing with children, giving rewards contingent to child's accomplishments, expression of affection and encouragement are likely to enhance the performance of children.

The last dimension in this questionnaire was about parents extending time, interest and resources. The ten items describe the type of involvement activities like the frequency in helping with homework, attending PTA, giving gifts and discussing about career opportunities.

The revised tool comprised eighty-eight statements concerning various aspects of parent Involvement on Likert's five-point scale.

3.6.1 Description of Final Tool

(I) Self-efficacy comprising of eighteen items, on a 5-point scale ranging from Strongly Disagree to Strongly Agree. Alpha reliability for the scale as used in the final study was .78.

(II) Role Construction with nine items on the same format ranging from Strongly Disagree to Strongly Agree and the Alpha Reliability being .80.

(III) Encouragement consisting of fourteen items on Likert Scale of Strongly Disagree to Strongly Agree with alpha reliability of .92.

(IV) Modelling Behaviours with nine items on five point scale of Not at all true to Completely True and achieving alpha reliability of .94.

(V) Reinforcement, which included thirteen items on Likert Scale Not at all true to Completely True and achieving alpha reliability .96.

(VI) Instructions comprising fifteen items in a scale of Not at all true to Completely True with alpha reliability of .92.

(VII) Investment of Time Interest and Resources comprising of ten items on a scale of Never, Sometimes, Rarely Often, Very often and achieving alpha reliability of .82.

Both parents (fathers and mothers were given identical tool. There was provision in the questionnaire for collecting personal information.

The investigator had already conveyed to parents about the purpose of the research and how it was to be filled during school P.T.A. session and their cooperation. Also assurance was given that information will be held in strict confidence. Those questionnaires were sent through students to their respective parents.

Statistical Treatment

In accordance with various objectives of the study, as mentioned in chapter 1, the data gathered was analysed and interpreted for arriving at sound conclusion and generalisation. The data was first tabulated and analysed using specific statistical techniques. The first step of analysis is to plan about the scoring procedure comprising of 65 statements. The scoring of responses was done by assigning integers 5, 4, 3, 2, 1 to positive statements and scores reversed for negative statements.

Other than the mean score, various other quantitative tools such as measures of dispersion (standard deviation) and Chi-Square test of Independence were used to interpret the tabulated data. The null hypotheses were verified.

4

Data Analysis and Interpretation

Research consists of systematic observation and description of the characteristics of properties of objects or events for the purpose of discovering relationships between variables. The ultimate purpose is to develop generalisation that may be used to explain phenomenon and future occurrences.

The data collected through the administration of tool on selected sample has no meaning unless these are analysed and interpreted in the light of objectives of the study for drawing sound conclusion and valid generalisation. Data analysis means logical interpretation of the tabulated material in order to determine the inherent facts.

According to Rummel (1996), the analysis and interpretation involves the objective material in the possession of the researcher and the subjective reactions and desires to derive from the data the inherent meaning in their relationships to the problem. Hence, data analysis as well as interpretation assumes paramount importance for conveying the essence of what the data reveal.

This chapter deals with the analysis and interpretation of the tabulated data in the light of objectives of the study.

Various quantitative tools such as measures of central tendency (mean), measures of dispersion (standard deviation) and Chi-square test between various sets of scores were used. The open ended questions were analysed qualitatively.

I. Questionnaire for Parents

Parental Involvement Project (PIP) Parent and Teacher questionnaire standardised by Kathleen Hoover- Dempsy (1995-97) and prepared by Darnale Webstel was adapted with modification and used as a tool for studying the involvement of parents in their children's education. The focus of the questionnaire was to study parents' perspective in the process to be involved in the education of their children.

As discussed in Chapter III, the questionnaire for parents comprised seven sub-scales that deal with motivational factors for getting involved, mechanisms most important to parents' thinking, decision-making and behaviours underlying these decisions to become involved in their children's education. The sub-scales included were Self-Efficacy, Role Construction, Encouragement, Modeling, Reinforcement, Instruction and Investment of Time Interest and Resources.

The objective wise analysis and interpretation of the results are being presented.

Objective-wise analysis is given as under:

Objective 1

To study the motivational factors for parents to be involved in the education of their children.

As discussed in chapter III, in order to study the process of parental involvement in senior secondary school students, the responses of 400 parents (200 fathers and 200 mothers) on Parental Involvement Questionnaire developed by Kathleen, Hoover-Dempsy were tabulated and analysed .The questionnaire was designed to permit the parents to indicate the extent of involvement in their children's academic activities. As discussed, the items related to motivational factors were from two sub-scales namely self-efficacy, and role construction. The focus of the sub-scales was on the extent to which parents believe that through their involvement they can exert positive influence on their children's educational outcome. It required the respondents to indicate how much they agreed or disagreed with the statements. The tools administered to corresponding fathers and mothers were identical and their response were scored in the same way. Scoring of the response was done by assigning numerical 5,4,3,2,1 to positive statements and 1,2,3,4,5 to the negative statements.

The maximum possible score for each item could be 5 and minimum score 1. Mean for each dimension was calculated from all statements under respective dimension and the total mean to find out the extent and belief of fathers for being involved in the education of their children. Table 4.1.1 indicates the scores of fathers and mothers for motivational factors for being involved in the education of their children.

Table 4.1.1: Parents' Belief about Self-efficacy and Parental Role Construction for Involvement in the Education of Children

Dimensions of Involvement	*No. of items*	*Max Score*	*Neutral score*	*Fathers Mean*	*SD*	*Mothers Mean*	*SD*
Self-efficacy	18	90	54	62.58	5.83	62.50	5.98
Role Construction	9	45	27	30.23.	6.08	29.94	4.06

I. Self-efficacy: Parent's sense of Self-efficacy is one of the major motivating factors for parents to become involved in the education of their children. Eighteen items in this dimension were meant to gauge parents' perception of self-efficacy that is their beliefs about general ability to influence child's developmental and educational outcome, about specific effectiveness in influencing the child's school learning and about their own influence for helping children succeed in school.

Table 4.1.1 indicates that the mean score on the dimension of self-efficacy for fathers was 62.58 and that of mothers were 62.50.

Both mean scores were above the minimum score of 18 and neutral score of 45 showing that fathers as well as mothers both had high Self-efficacy beliefs. It implies that both the parents perceived themselves to be confident about helping their wards, they knew how to supervise their child's work and they were also confident of seeking cooperation from school regarding their ward's academic progress. Fig. 4.1 depicts the same trend.

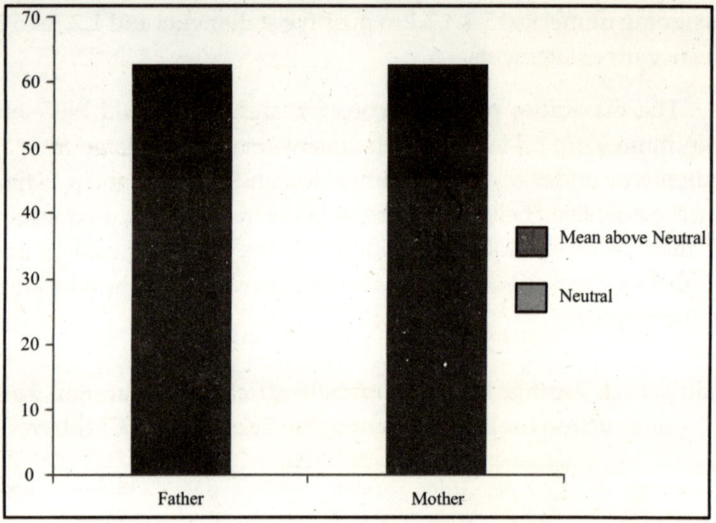

Fig. 4.1. Self-efficacy of Fathers and Mothers.

II. Parent's Role Construction: One major contributor to parents' positive decisions about being involved in their children's education is to be found in the construction of parental role. Parents' ideas about child rearing and appropriate role in supporting children's education at home appear to constitute important specific component about involvement in their children's education. The items in this sub-scale namely parents' role construction consisted of nine items which dealt with parent's beliefs about their roles and responsibilities towards children: what do parents believe they are supposed to do in relationships to children's education.

The mean score in this dimension for fathers was 30.23 and that of mothers was 29.94. Though it was only marginally above the neutral score of 24, it indicated that fathers and mothers were aware of their roles as parents and knew their responsibilities towards their children's education. They felt it as their duty to communicate with teachers regularly and volunteer for school activities, explain tough assignments to their children etc. These findings have been depicted in Fig. 4.2.

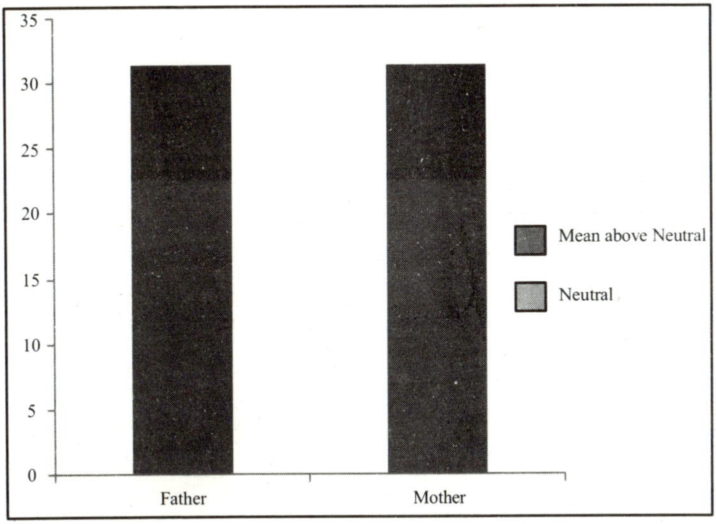

Fig. 4.2. Role Construction by Fathers and Mothers.

Objective 2

To study the extent of the use of mechanisms through which parental involvement influence children's educational outcome.

Parents may engage various psychological mechanism when they enact involvement activities. According to Kathleen Hoover-Demsey (1997), the most important of such mechanism for being involved are providing encouragement, exhibiting modeling behaviour, providing positive reinforcement and imparting instructions regarding educational activities of children.

Mothers and fathers included in the sample were asked to rate the items related to the mechanism on a five-point scale. Results along with other relevant details are given in Table 4.1.2.

Table 4.1.2: Extent of Parental Involvement Mechanism for Education of their Children

Dimensions of Involvement	*No. of items*	*Max Score*	*Neutral score*	*Fathers Mean*	*SD*	*Mothers Mean*	*SD*
Encouragement	14	70	42	52.32	5.82	55.31	6.88
Modelling	9	5	27	33.90	7.07	33.49	5.16
Reinforcement	13	65	39	47.81	5.21	46.50	7.21
Instruction	15	75	45	56.52	7.74	55.54	7.67

(a) Encouragement: Emotional support in the form of warmth and encouragement are basic foundations of quality of parent child relationship. Encouragement is another important psychological mechanism of parental involvement. The scale included 14 items that focused on explicit parental support and encouragement for student's interest, aptitude and approach towards school and learning. As Table 4.1.2 indicates, Mean score for fathers was 52.32 and that of corresponding mothers was 55.31. Here, the score obtained were higher than the neutral score of 42 with mothers' score comparatively higher than that of fathers. The same is shown in Fig. 4.3.

(b) Modeling Behaviour: Modelling is another mechanism used during the process of involvement. There were nine items in this dimension ranging from not at all true to completely true format related to modeling behaviours of parents; how they set examples for their children by showing how to solve problems, how to enjoy learning new things etc.

The mean score in this dimension for fathers was 33.90 and that of mothers was 33.49. Since the scores were above the minimum of nine and neutral value of 27, it indicates that parents were aware of the need to set examples for children and show their wards how to solve problems, how to figure things out and learn. The same is illustrated in Fig. 4.4.

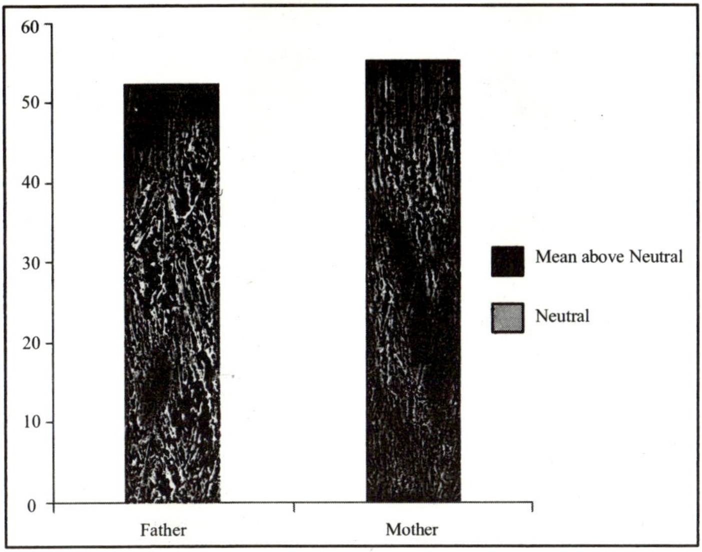

Fig. 4.3: Encouragement given by Fathers and Mothers.

(c) Reinforcement: Positive reinforcement contributes to developing and maintaining student attributes associated with positive learning outcome.

Thirteen items in this dimension were meant to study the pattern of reinforcement and appreciation as provided by parents to children.

Table 4.1.2 indicates the mean score in the dimension of reinforcement for fathers as 47.81 and that of mothers as 46.50. Again the high scores for fathers as well as mothers imply both parents perceived themselves as providing positive reinforcement to children's education with fathers' score slightly more than that of corresponding mothers. This has been demonstrated through Fig. 4.

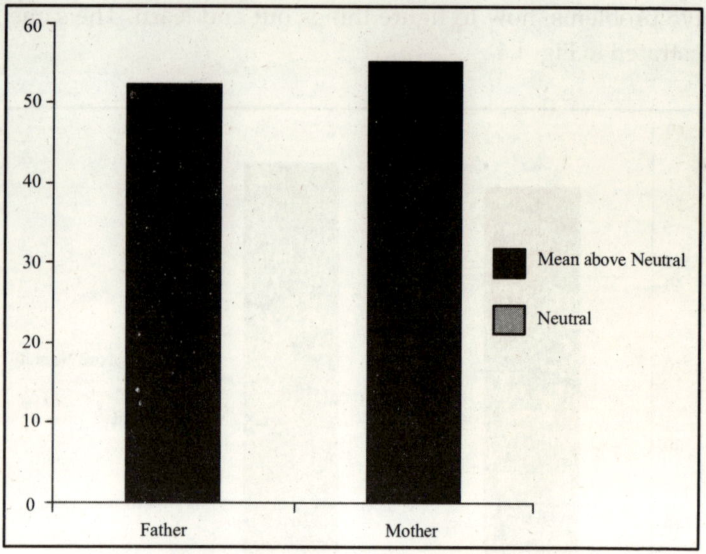

Fig. 4.4. Modelling Behaviours by Fathers and Mothers.

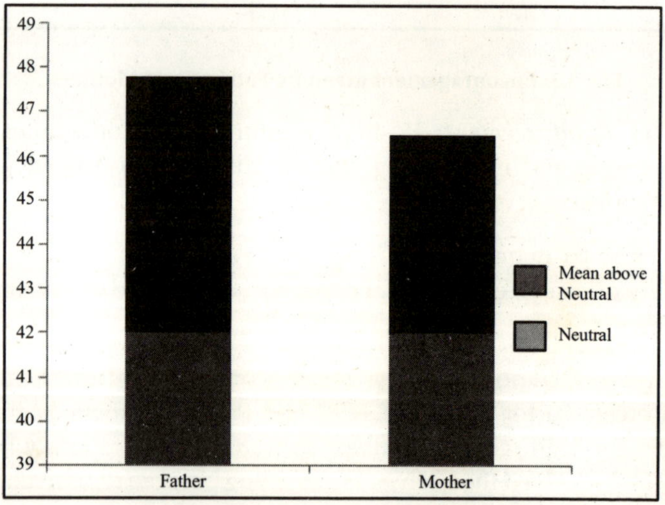

Fig. 4.5. Reinforcement by Fathers and Mothers.

(d) Instruction: Parental instruction emerges in social interaction between parent and child as a mechanism during involvement activities as they engage in shared thinking related to learning strategies and in direct instructional strategies. The scale included 15 items (e.g., "We teach our child how to check homework as s(he) goes along;" "We teach our child to ask questions when s(he) doesn't understand something"). The mean score in the dimension of instruction for fathers was 56.52 and that of mothers was 55.54, which were much above the neutral score of 45, confirming that parents provide valuable instructions to their wards. These findings are depicted in Fig. 4.6.

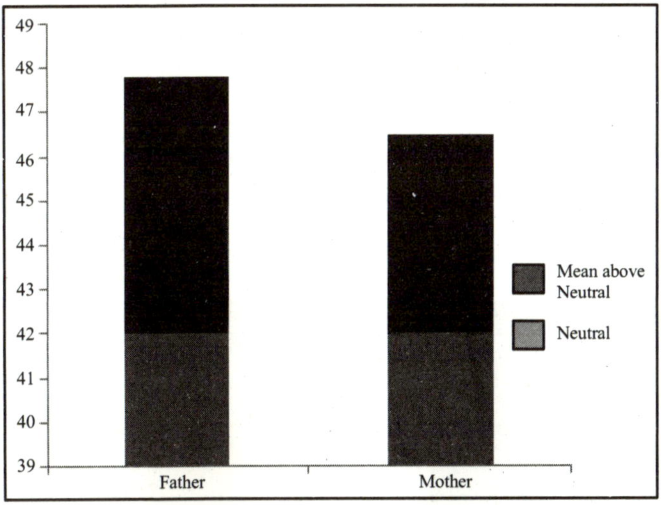

Fig. 4.6. Instructions given by Fathers and Mothers.

Objective 3

To study the extent of time, interest and resources by parents for being involved in the education of children. Parents' choice of being involved in the education of children is influenced by their time, interest and resources they have had for getting involved in education of children.

Investment of Time, Interest and Resources: The last dimension in this questionnaire was about parents extending time, interest and resources for education of children. The items in this dimension were meant to study how much time, resources and interest are utilised by parents in the day-to-day activities of children. The ten items describe the type of involvement activities like the frequency in helping with home work, attending PTA, giving gifts and discussing about career opportunities.

Table 4.1.3. Extent of Time, Interest and Resources by Parents for Education of Children

Dimensions of Involvement	*No. of items*	*Max Score*	*Neutral score*	*Fathers Mean*	*SD*	*Mothers Mean*	*SD*
Investment of time, resource	10	50	30	36.97	2.83	37.10	6.04
Total	**88**	**440**	**264**	**321.33**	**40.58**	**320.38**	**43.00**

The mean score as depicted in Table 4.1.3 for fathers and mothers was 36.97 and 37.10 respectively.

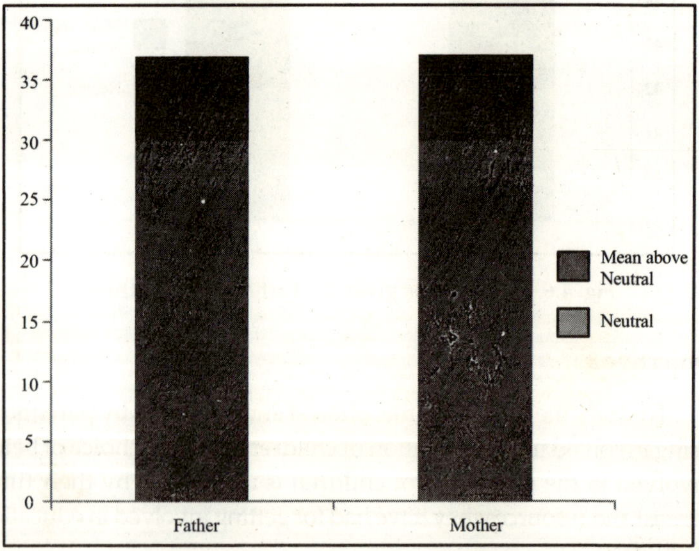

Fig. 4.7. Investment by Fathers and Mothers with respect to the extent of time, energy and resources.

The scores were much above the minimum value of 10 and slightly above the neutral value of 30, which reflect fathers and mothers have been proved to be investing time to attend PTA, special events in school, go on outing with family and discuss with children about career opportunities. They were ready to invest resources to a limited extent. Fig. 4.7 illustrates the same.

Overall involvement in terms of the means of the total obtained scores in all dimensions of parental involvement for fathers and mothers was also calculated. The same is given in Table 4.1.4 and graphical representation in Fig. 4.8.

Table 4.1.4. Involvement of Fathers and Mothers with Respect to Total Score on all Dimensions

Sample Group	*N*	*Max score*	*Neutral Score*	*Mean*	*S.D*
Fathers	200	440	264	321.33	40.58
Mothers	200	440	264	320.38	43.00

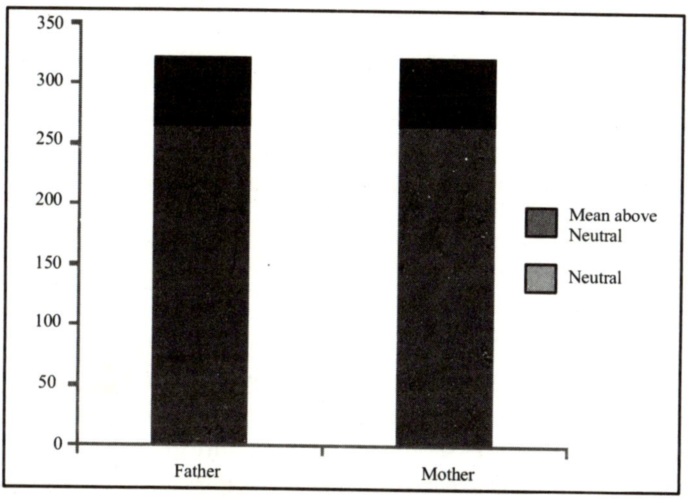

Fig. 4.8. Overall Involvement.

As reflected from Table 4.1.4 and Figure 4.8, the mean score of fathers was 321.33 and mothers 320.38 regarding overall involvement with children. The scores were higher than the minimum score of 88 and neutral score of 264. Hence, the perception of the respondent groups were somewhat inclined towards involvement in academic pursuit of children. Since the scores were higher than the neutral score of 264, it may be inferred that fathers as well as mothers of senior secondary school children had confidence in their abilities to deal with children's activities, were aware of the roles and responsibilities, were willing to set examples for the children and agreed they provide encouragement, positive reinforcement valuable instructions and engage them in such involvement activities.

Objective 4

To make school-wise comparison of perception of fathers regarding motivational factors in the education of children.

To compare the perceptions of fathers regarding the involvement it was felt Chi-Square would be suitable statistical method. Chi-Square is based on the assumption that the data may be such that it can be classified into "mutually exclusive categories" (Lindquist 1940 p. 30). It may be used for the calculation of contingency coefficient which gives the numerical value of relationship between two variables. This statistics compare the observed frequencies (*fo*) for each category to frequencies that would be expected (*fe*) if the null hypothesis is true. The formula for calculation is,

$$\chi^2 = \sum_{i=1} (fo - fe)^2 / fe$$

To prepare a 3 × 4 contingency table, firstly scores in each dimension was arranged into three categories – roughly equal in size in all categories. The respondents were placed in these categories based on the responses scored as per procedure given in chapter III. The scores of fathers in each dimension were arranged in ascending order, roughly 1/3 from the bottom formed the top group 'Low'. The second 1/3 from the bottom formed the second group Medium and the top 1/3 formed the top group Chi-Square was computed for each motivational factor to test the following hypotheses.

H_0.1.1. There is no significant difference in the extent of belief of fathers of children studying in Private, Aided Central and

Government schools about their Self-efficacy for being involved in the education of children.

H_0 1.2. There is no significant difference in the extent of belief of fathers of children studying in Private Aided, Central and Government schools about their roles and responsibilities for being involved in the education of children.

(a) Self-efficacy

In order to study parents' sense of self-efficacy with special reference to parental involvement, the self-efficacy component of parent questionnaire was studied among fathers, whose children study in four types of schools namely Private, Aided, Central and Government. The same is given in Contingency Table 4.1.5 .

Table 4.1.5. 3 × 4 Contingency Table: Comparison of Perception of Fathers' Self-efficacy

Self-efficacy	*Type of Schools*				
	Private	*Aided*	*Central*	*Govt.*	*Total*
Low	13 (26.0)	13 (26.0)	24 (48.0)	16 (32.0)	66 (33.0)
Medium	20 (40.0)	22 (44.0)	14 (28.0)	20 (40.0)	76 (38.0)
High	17 (34.0)	15 (30.0)	12 (24.0)	14 (28.0)	58 (29.0)
Total	**50** **(100.0)**	**50** **(100.0)**	**50** **(100.0)**	**50** **(100.0)**	**200** **(100.0)**

The figures given in parenthesis indicate percentages.
χ^2 = 7.70; *df* = 6; *insignificant.*

Since the value of Chi-Square 7.70 is less than its critical value of 12.59 for 6df at .05 level, it is not significant. Hence, the hypothesis that there is no significant difference in the perception of fathers about self-efficacy is accepted. Self-efficacy of fathers of children studying in Private, Aided, Central and Government schools did not vary. All fathers irrespective of schools, where their children studied perceived them to have self-efficacy in rearing and caring of children.

(b) Role Construction

The items in this dimension were meant to gauge the perception of fathers about awareness of roles and responsibilities as parents. For calculation of Chi-Square value, the same procedure was adopted to test null hypothesis. The same is given in Contingency Table 4.1.6.

Table 4.1.6. 3 × 4 Contingency Table: Comparison of Perceptions of Fathers' Role Construction

Level of Role Construction	*Type of Schools*				
	Private	*Aided*	*Central*	*Govt.*	*Total*
Low	16 (32.0)	18 (36.0)	17 (34.0)	19 (38.0)	70 (35.0)
Medium	13 (26.0)	13 (26.0)	19 (38.0)	13 (26.0)	58 (29.0)
High	21 (42.0)	19 (38.0)	14 (28.0)	18 (36.0)	72 (36.0)
Total	**50 (100.0)**	**50 (100.0)**	**50 (100.0)**	**50 (100.0)**	**200 (100.0)**

The figures given in parenthesis indicate percentages.
df = 6; χ^2 = 3.59 *df* = 6; insignificant.

Chi-Square value of 3.59 is insignificant at .05 level. Hence, the hypothesis that there is no significant difference in the belief of fathers of children studying in Private Aided, Central and Government schools about the roles and responsibilities for being involved in education of children is accepted.

Objective 5

To make school-wise comparison of fathers with respect to the use of mechanism through which parental involvement influence children's educational outcome.

In order to realise the above objective, Chi-Square was used and the following hypotheses were tested:

$H_0$1.3. There is no significant difference in the extent of belief of fathers of children studying in Private, Aided, Central and Government schools about the mechanism of encouragement in education of children.

H_0 1.4. There is no significant difference in the extent of belief of fathers of children studying in Private, Aided, Central and Government schools about the mechanism of modelling behaviours in education of children.

$H_0$1.5. There is no significant difference in the extent of belief of fathers of children studying in Private, central and Government schools about the use of mechanism of reinforcement in the education of children.

$H_0$1.6. There is no significant difference in the extent of belief of fathers of children studying in Private, Aided, Central and Government schools about the mechanism of instructions in the education of children.

$H_0$1.7. There is no significant difference in the extent of belief of fathers of children studying in Private Aided, Central and Government schools about investing time, resources and interest in the education of children.

(a) Encouragement

Emotional support in the form of encouragement is said to have a positive influence on children. A comparison was drawn to test the hypothesis that there is no significant difference in the extent of belief of fathers of children studying in Private, Aided Central and Government schools about encouragement.

The results are given in Table 4.1.7.

Table 4.1.7. 3 × 4 Contingency Table: Comparison of Mechanism of Encouragement by Fathers

Level of Encouragement	*Type of Schools*				
	Private	*Aided*	*Central*	*Govt.*	*Total*
Low	16 (32.0)	17 (34.0)	14 (28.0)	22 (44.0)	69 (34.5)
Medium	18 (36.0)	18 (36.0)	20 (40.0)	16 (32.0)	72 (36.0)
High	16 (32.0)	15 (30.0)	16 (32.0)	12 (24.0)	59 (29.5)
Total	**50** **(100.0)**	**50** **(100.0)**	**50** **(100.0)**	**50** **(100.0)**	**200** **(100.0)**

The figures given in parenthesis indicate percentages.
$\chi^2 = 3.18$; $df = 6$; insignificant.

The value of Chi-Square is 3.18 which is again less than critical value for 6df and therefore insignificant. Hence, the hypothesis that there is no significant difference in the extent of belief of fathers about encouragement is accepted. Encouragement provided by fathers of children studying in Private, Aided, Central and Government schools about developing confidence, valuing traditions, open to new ideas, etc., do not differ.

(b) Modelling Behaviour

Parents set examples to children through their own behaviour of showing how to learn new things, how to tackle problems etc.

Comparison of modeling behaviour of fathers yielded significant results as given in Table 4.1.8.

Table 4.1.8. 3 × 4 Contingency Table: Comparison of Mechanism of Modelling Behaviour of Fathers

Level of Encouragement	*Type of Schools*				
	Private	*Aided*	*Central*	*Govt.*	*Total*
Low	16 (32.0)	17 (34.0)	14 (28.0)	22 (44.0)	69 (34.5)

Medium	18	18	20	16	72
	(36.0)	(36.0)	(40.0)	(32.0)	(36.0)
High	16	15	16	12	59
	(32.0)	(30.0)	(32.0)	(24.0)	(29.5)
Total	**50**	**50**	**50**	**50**	**200**
	(100.0)	**(100.0)**	**(100.0)**	**(100.0)**	**(100.0)**

The figures given in parenthesis indicate percentages.
χ^2 = 21.3; *df* = 6; significant at .01 level.

Chi-Square value of 21.38 is much greater than its critical value (12.59) for 6df and it is significant at .01 level. Hence, the hypothesis that there is no significant difference in the perception of fathers about the extent of modeling behaviours exhibited by them is rejected. It implies that fathers of children studying in Private, Aided, Central and Government schools differ with respect to their perception of modeling behaviour. They differ in their way they set examples for their children.

(c) Reinforcement

Appreciation and reinforcement contribute to the overall development of children. Table 4.1.9 compares the perception of fathers with respect to this mechanism of parental involvement.

Table 4.1.9. 3 × 4 Contingency Table: Comparison of Mechanism of Reinforcement by Fathers

Level of	*Type of Schools*				
Reinforcement	*Private*	*Aided*	*Central*	*Govt.*	*Total*
Low	24	18	10	17	69
	(48.0)*	(36.0	(20.0)	(34.0)	(34.5)
Medium	9	24	15	14	62
	(18.0)	(48.0)	(30.0)	(28.0	(31.0)
High	17	8	25	19	69
	(34.0)	(16.0	(50.0)	(38.0	(34.5)
Total	**50**	**50**	**50**	**50**	**200**
	(100.0)	**(100.0)**	**(100.0)**	**(100.0)**	**(100.0)**

The figures given in parenthesis indicate percentages.
χ^2 = 21.89; *df* = 6; significant at .01 level.

Table 4.1.9 shows that Chi-Square value of 21.89 is significant at .01 level. Hence, the hypothesis that there is no significant difference in the perception of fathers whose children studying in various types of schools in providing reinforcement is rejected. Perception of fathers differed significantly with regards to appreciation and positive reinforcement to their children.

(d) Instruction

Parents may differ in the way they impart instruction to their wards regarding how to plan their studies, tackle problems in daily lives, plan for future etc.

Table 4.1.10 shows the value of Chi-Square in this dimension.

3 × 4 Contingency Table: Comparison of Mechanism of Instruction.

Level of Instruction	*Type of Schools*				
	Private	*Aided*	*Central*	*Govt.*	*Total*
Low	19 (38.0)	21 (42.0)	11 (22.0)	15 (30.0)	66 (33.0)
Medium	14 (28.0)	15 (30.0)	18 (36.0)	25 (50.0)	72 (36.0)
High	17 (34.0)	14 (28.0)	21 (42.0)	10 (20.0)	62 (31.0)
Total	**50** **(100.0)**	**50** **(100.0)**	**50** **(100.0)**	**50** **(100.0)**	**200** **(100.0)**

The figures given in parenthesis indicate percentages.
$\chi^2 = 11.88$; $df = 6$; significant at .05 level.

Chi-Square value in the above Table is 11.88 for 6df which is significant at .05. Hence, the hypothesis that there is no significant difference in the perception of fathers, whose children study in different type of schools about the way of imparting instruction is rejected. It implies the extent of imparting instruction towards by fathers whose children study in different type of schools regarding how to plan work, do home work, have an attitude towards studies etc. were not similar.

Objective 6

- To make school-wise comparison of fathers with respect to investment of time, interest and resources in the education of children.
- Investment of Time, Interest and Resources.

The perception of fathers with reference to extending their time resources and interest for their children has been tabulated in Table 4.1.11.

Table 4.1.11. 3 × 4 Contingency Table: Comparison of Perception of Fathers about the Investment of Time, Interest and Resources.

Level of Investment	*Type of Schools*				
	Private	*Aided*	*Central*	*Govt.*	*Total*
Low	13 (26.0)	13 (26.0)	24 (48.0)	16 (32.0)	66 (33.0)
Medium	20 (40.0)	22 (44.0)	14 (28.0)	20 (40.0)	76 (38.0)
High	17 (34)	15 (30.0)	12 (24.0)	14 (28.0)	58 (29.0)
Total	**50 (100.0)**	**50 (100.0)**	**50 (100.0)**	**50 (100.0)**	**200 (100.0)**

The figures given in parenthesis indicate percentage.
χ^2 =19.10; df = 6; significant at .01 level.

Chi-Square value of 19.10 is significant at .05 level. Therefore, the hypothesis that there is no significant difference in the perception of fathers of children studying in Private, Aided, Central and Government schools about extending time resources and interest in the education of children is rejected. It is obvious that the extent of investment of time, resources etc. by fathers for children studying in different type of schools were not same.

Objective 7

To make school-wise comparison of motivational factors for mothers involved in the education of children.

As in the case of fathers, scores of mothers on Self-efficacy and role construction in four types of schools were compared. Also the following hypotheses were tested.

$H_0$2.1. There is no significant difference in the extent of belief of mothers of children studying in Private, Aided Central and Government schools about their Self-efficacy for being involved in the education of children.

$H_0$2.2. There is no significant difference in the extent of belief of mothers of children studying in Private Aided, Central and Government schools about their roles and responsibilities for being involved in the education of their children.

(a) Self-efficacy

Mothers' perceptions of their ability to perform their duty as parents successfully was compared, the result of which is given in Table 4.2.1.

Table 4.2.1. 3 × 4 Contingency Table: Comparison of Perception of Mothers' Self-efficacy

Level of Self Efficacy	*Type of Schools*				
	Private	*Aided*	*Central*	*Govt.*	*Total*
Low	16	16	19	20	71
	(32.0)	(32.0)	(38.0)	(40.0)	(35.5)
Medium	18	17	13	19	67
	(36.0)	(34.0)	(26.0)	(38.0)	(33.5)
High	16	17	18	11	62
	(32.0)	(34.0)	(36.0)	(22.0)	(31.0)
Total	**50**	**50**	**50**	**50**	**200**
	(100.0)	**(100.0)**	**(100.0)**	**(100.0)**	**(100.0)**

The figures given in parenthesis indicate percentages.
χ^2 = 3.82; *df* = 6; insignificant.

Chi-Square value of 3.82 is insignificant for 6df. Hence, the hypothesis that there is no significant difference in the perception of mothers of children studying in Private, Aided Central and

Government schools about their self-efficacy in terms of parental involvement is retained. It implies that irrespective of schools where children studied, mothers held similar views about their efficacy in the education of children.

(b) Role Construction

The items in the next scale dealt with mothers' belief about the roles as parents and the awareness about the responsibilities towards children. Comparison of perceptions of mothers with respect to different type of schools in which their children study did not show significant statistical difference. Table 4.2.2 illustrates this aspect.

Table 4.2.2. 3 × 4 Contingency Table: Comparison of Perception of Mothers' Role Construction

Level of Role Construction	*Type of Schools*				
	Private	*Aided*	*Central*	*Govt.*	*Total*
Low	15 (30)	17 (34)	17 (34)	28 (56.0)	77 (154.0)
Medium	16 (32.0)	14 (28.0)	17 (34.0)	9 (18.0	56 (28.0)
High	19 (38.0)	19 (38.0)	16 (32.0)	13 (26.0	67 (33.5)
Total	**50** **(100.0)**	**50** **(100.0)**	**50** **(100.0)**	**50** **(100.0)**	**200** **(100.0)**

The figures given in parenthesis indicate percentages.
$\chi^2 = 9.66$; $df = 6$; insignificant.

Chi-Square value of 9.66 is not significant. Hence, the hypothesis that there is no significant difference in the perception of mothers of children studying in Private, Aided Central and Government schools about role construction is retained. Mothers' awareness about the duties as parents was more or less the same with respect to the type of schools in which children were studying.

Objective 8

To make school-wise comparison of mothers with respect to the use of mechanism through which parental involvement influence children's educational outcome.

In order to realise the objective, Chi-Square was used and the following hypotheses were tested.

H_0 2.3. There is no significant difference in the extent of belief of mothers of children studying in Private, Aided Central and Government schools about the encouragement in the education of children.

H_0 2.4. There is no significant difference in extent of belief of mothers of children studying in Private, Aided, Central and Government schools about the modelling behaviour to influence the education of children.

H_0 2.5. There is no significant difference in the extent of belief of mothers of children studying in Private, central and Government schools about the reinforcement to influence the education of children.

H_0 2.6. There is no significant difference in the extent of belief of mothers of children studying in Private, Aided, Central and Government schools about the extent of use of mechanism of instruction to influence the education of children.

(a) Encouragement

Comparison of mothers' self-reported encouragement was studied, the result of which is illustrated in Table 4.2.3.

Table 4.2.3. 3 × 4 Contingency Table: Comparison of Perception of Mothers' Encouragement

Level of Encouragement	*Type of Schools*				
	Private	*Aided*	*Central*	*Govt.*	*Total*
Low	18 (36.0)	18 (36.0)	16 (32.0)	22 (44.0)	74 (37.0)

Medium	19	14	19	10	62
	(38.0)	(28.0)	(38.0)	(20.0)	(31.0)
High	13	18	15	16	64
	(26.0)	(38.0)	(30.0)	(32.0)	(32.0)
Total	**50**	**50**	**50**	**50**	**200**
	(100.0)	**(100.0)**	**(100.0)**	**(100.0)**	**(100.0)**

The figures given in parenthesis indicate percentages.
χ^2 = 5.82; ; *df* = 6; insignificant.

The above comparison did not show significant statistical difference (Chi-Square value is 5.82) which is less than its critical value of 12.59 for 6df. Hence, the hypothesis that there is no significant difference in the extent of belief of mothers of children studying in Private, Aided Central and Government schools about the mechanics of encouragement. The extent of belief of mothers regarding the encouragement they provide to children did not differ with respect to type of schools where their children study.

(b) Modeling Behaviour

In various ways, mothers set example for their children. Comparison of modelling behaviour of mothers yielded significant Chi-Square value, which is illustrated in the Table 4.2.4.

Table 4.2.4. 3x4 Contingency Table: Comparison of Mechanism of Modelling Behaviour by Mothers

Level of	*Type of Schools*				
Modelling	*Private*	*Aided*	*Central*	*Govt.*	*Total*
Low	24	13	10	18	65
	(48.0)	(26.0)	(20.0)	(36.0)	(32.5)
Medium	16	21	21	22	80
	(32.0)	(42.0)	(42.0)	(44.0)	(40.0)
High	10	16	19	10	55
	(20.0)	(32.0)	(38.0)	(20.0)	(27.5)
Total	**50**	**50**	**50**	**50**	**200**
	(100.0)	**(100.0)**	**(100.0)**	**(100.0)**	**(100.0)**

The figures given in parenthesis indicate percentages.
df = 6; χ^2 = 12.40; significant at .05 level.

Table 4.2.4 showed statistical difference (Chi-Square is 12.40) which is significant at .05 level. Hence, the hypothesis that no significant difference in the extent of belief of mothers of children studying in Private, Aided Central and Government schools about the mechanism of modelling behaviours as rejected. The level of awareness of mothers about the need to set example for children varied with respect to the type of school in which the children study.

(c) Reinforcement

Positive reinforcement provided by parents can have an impact on children.

An attempt was made to compare mothers' perceived reinforcement given to children.

Table 4.2.5. 3 × 4 Contingency Table: Comparison of Mechanism of Reinforcement by Mothers

Level of Reinforcement	*Type of Schools*				
	Private	*Aided*	*Central*	*Govt.*	*Total*
Low	27 (54.0)	18 (36.0)	18 (36.0)	23 (46.0)	86 (43.0)
Medium	8 (16.0)	22 (44.0)	19 (38.0)	14 (28.0	63 (31.5)
High	15 (30.0)	10 (20.0)	13 (26.0)	13 (26.0	51 (25.5)
Total	**50** **(100.0)**	**50** **(100.0)**	**50** **(100.0)**	**50** **(100.0)**	**200** **(100.0)**

The figures given in parenthesis indicate percentages.
χ^2 = 11.00; *df* = 6; insignificant.

Since the value of Chi-Square is insignificant (11.00), the hypothesis that no significant difference in the mechanism of reinforcement by mothers whose children study in Private, Aided, Central and Government schools as retained. In other words, mothers whose children study in different schools did not differ with respect to the extent of reinforcement to cnildren.

(d) Instructions

Mothers impart instruction to their wards about various aspects like how to cope with studies, uphold values etc. Perception of mothers with the mechanism of instruction was compared. Table 4.2.6 shows the results.

Table 4.2.6. 3 × 4 Contingency Table: Comparison of Perception of Mechanism of Instructions by Mothers.

Level of Role Efficacy	*Type of Schools*				
	Private	*Aided*	*Central*	*Govt.*	*Total*
Low	18 (36.0)	18 (36.0)	16 (32.0)	23 (36.0)	75 (37.5)
Medium	13 (26.0)	20 (40.0)	26 (42.0)	16 (32.0)	75 (37.5)
High	19 (38.0)	12 (24.0)	8 (16.0)	11 (22.0)	50 (25.0)
Total	**50 (100.0)**	**50 (100.0)**	**50 (100.0)**	**50 (100.0)**	**200 (100.0)**

The figures given in parenthesis indicate percentages.
χ^2 =12.05; –6; significant at .01 level.

Chi-Square value of 12.05 is significant. Hence, the hypothesis that there is no significant difference in the imparting of instruction by mothers of children studying in Private, Aided, Central and Government as rejected. It implies that instruction to children did differ with respect to the type of school.

Objective 9

To make school-wise comparison of mothers with respect to their investment of time, interest and resources in the education of their children.

Investment of Time, Interest Resources:

Parents involve them in the activities of children by assisting in their homework, taking them out, buying gifts etc. A comparison of mothers of children studying in Aided, Private, Central and

Government school was done to find any significant difference existed with respect to the investment of time, interest and resources and also the following hypothesis was tested.

H_0 2.7. There is no significant difference in the extent of belief of mothers of children studying in Private Aided, Central and Government schools about investing time, resources and interest in the education of their children. Table 4.2.7 illustrates the results.

Table 4.2.7. 3 × 4 Contingency Table: Comparison of Mothers' Investment of Time, Interest and Resources

Level of Investment	*Type of Schools*				
	Private	*Aided*	*Central*	*Govt.*	*Total*
Low	22 (11.0)	15 (30.0)	16 (32.0)	19 (38.0)	72 (36.0)
Medium	9 (18.0)	23 (46.0)	17 (34.0)	20 (40.0)	69 (34.5)
High	19 (38.0)	12 (24.0)	17 (34.0)	11 (22.0)	59 (29.5)
Total	**50** **(100.0)**	**50** **(100.0)**	**50** **(100.0)**	**50** **(100.0)**	**200** **(100.0)**

The figures given in parenthesis indicate percentages.
χ^2 = 11.00; *df* =6; insignificant.

Chi-Square value of 11.00 is insignificant. Hence, the hypothesis that there is no significant difference in the involvement of mothers in terms of investment of time, interest and resources is accepted. It can be interpreted that the extent of investment of time, interest and resources by mothers for children studying in different types of schools were the same.

Objective 10

To find if fathers differ from mothers with respect to the process of involvement in the education of children.

Since one of the chief objectives was to find any significant difference between fathers and mothers in the involvement, comparison on seven dimensions was studied and the following hypotheses were tested.

H_0 3.1. There is no significant difference between fathers and mothers with respect to the extent of belief of Self-efficacy for involvement in the education of children.

H_0 3.2. There is no significant difference between fathers and mothers with respect to the extent of belief of role construction for involvement in the education of children.

H_0 3.3. There is no significant difference between fathers and mothers with respect to the extent of use of mechanism of encouragement in the education of children.

H_0 3.4. There is no significant difference between fathers and mothers with respect to the extent of use of mechanism of modeling behaviour in the education of children.

H_0 3.5. There is no significant difference between fathers and mothers with respect to the extent of use of mechanism of reinforcement in the education of children.

H_0 3.6. There is no significant difference between fathers and mothers with respect to the extent of use of mechanism of instruction in the education of children.

H_0 3.7. There is no significant difference between fathers and mothers with respect to the investment of time, interest and resources in the education of children.

For the purpose of comparison, Chi-Square test of independence was used. As mentioned earlier, it is a useful application to investigate the relationship between traits or attributes which can be classified into two or more categories. It explains whether two attributes are associated.

Dimension-wise analysis is given as under:

Self-efficacy

Self-efficacy of parent is an important determinant of involvement. Parent's sense of Self-efficacy refers to the degree to which the parent feels s(he) make any difference in children's learning.

An attempt was made to find whether the perception of mothers and fathers sense of Self-efficacy with specific reference to parental involvement were similar. Table 4.3.1 shows the result.

Table 4.3.1. 3 × 3 Contingency Table: Comparison of Perception of Fathers and Mothers with respect to the sense of Self-efficacy in Parental Involvement

Mothers' Self-efficacy	*Fathers' Self-efficacy* Low	Medium	High	Total
Low	34	20	17	71
	(51.5)	(26.3)	(29.3)	(35.5)
Medium	16	37	34	67
	(24.2	(48.7)	(24.1)	(33.5)
High	16	19	27	62
	(24.2)	(25)	(46.6)	(31)
Total	**66**	**76**	**58**	**200**
	(100.0)	**(100.0)**	**(100.0)**	**(100.0)**

The figures given in parenthesis indicate percentages.
χ^2 = 22.01; *df* = 4; Significant at .01 level.

The obtained Chi-Square value of 22.01 is significant at .01 level. It implies there is significant difference between fathers and mothers with respect to the perception of Self-efficacy. The null hypothesis H_0 3.1 is rejected. It is apparent that the self-efficacy beliefs regarding parental involvement of mothers and fathers differed from each other.

Role Construction

Parents are likely to get involved in their child's education to the extent they see it as part of the role or 'job' as it were. A comparison of the extent of fathers' and mothers' involvement in terms of the construction of parental roles was made and the result is depicted in Table 4.3.2.

Table 4.3.2. 3 × 3 Contingency Table: Comparison of Perception of Fathers and Mothers with respect to the sense of Role Construction

Mothers' role Construction	*Fathers' Role Construction*			
	Low	*Medium*	*High*	*Total*
Low	42	15	20	77
	(60)	(25.9)	(27.8)	38.5
Medium	12	28	16	56
	(17.1)	(48.3)	(22.2)	28
High	16	15	36	67
	(22.9)	(25.9)	(50)	33.5
Total	**70**	**58**	**72**	**200**
	(100.0)	**(100.0)**	**(100.0)**	**(100.0)**

The figures given in parenthesis indicate percentages.
$\chi^2 = 34.5$; $df = 4$; significant at .01 level.

Table 4.3.2 indicating involvement in terms of role construction showed significant statistical difference at .01 level. Hence, the hypothesis that there is no significant difference between fathers and mothers in the extent of involvement in terms of role construction is rejected.The way in which fathers and mothers perceived their roles as parents was not similar.

Encouragement

A comparison of mechanism of involvement with respect to encouragement was made between fathers and mothers. The result is illustrated in Table 4.3.3

Table 4.3.3. 3 × 3 Contingency Table: Comparison of the Extent of Use of Mechanism of Encouragement by Fathers and Mothers

Mothers' Encouragement	*Fathers' Encouragement*			
	Low	*Medium*	*High*	*Total*
Low	47	15	12	74
	(68.1)	(20.8)	(20.3)	37
Medium	7	35	20	62
	(10.1)	(48.6)	(33.9)	31

High	15 (21.7)	22 (30.6)	27 (45.9)	64 32
Total	**69** **(100.0)**	**75** **(100.0)**	**59** **(100.0)**	**200** **(100.0)**

The figures given in parenthesis indicate percentages.
$\chi^2 = 50.42$; *df* = 6; significant at .01 level.

Since the Chi-Square value is 50.42 which is significant at .01 level, H_0 3.3 is rejected confirming that the difference in respect of encouragement by fathers and mothers is significant and the difference is not by chance.

Modeling Behaviour

The next contingency table compares the perception of mothers and fathers about the modeling behaviour.

Table 4.3.4. 3 × 3 Contingency Table: Comparison of Extent of Modelling Behaviour by Fathers and Mothers

Mother's Modelling Behaviour	*Father's Modelling Behaviour*			
	Low	*Medium*	*High*	*Total*
Low	35 (57.4)	21 (27.3)	9 (14.5)	65 32.5
Medium	19 (31.1)	43 (55.8)	18 (29.1)	80 40
High	7 (11.5)	13 (16.9)	35 (56.5)	55 27.5
Total	**61** **(100.0)**	**77** **(100.0)**	**62** **(100.0)**	**200** **(100.0)**

The figures given in parenthesis indicate percentages.
$\chi^2 = 54.0$; *df* = 4; significant at .01 level.

Considering the above scores, significant difference could be noticed. Therefore, the hypothesis H_0 3.4 which states that there is no significant difference between fathers and mothers in the perception of involvement in terms of modeling behaviour is not accepted. It is evident that fathers differ from mothers in the way they set examples for children.

Reinforcement: Comparison of perceived reinforcement showed significant difference at .01 level implying the perception of fathers and mothers regarding the use of mechanism of reinforcement varied. The same is illustrated in Table 4.3.

Table 4.3.5. 3 × 3 Contingency Table: Comparison of the Extent of use of Mechanism of Reinforcement by Fathers and Mothers

Mother's Reinforcement	*Fathers' Reinforcement*			
	Low	*Medium*	*High*	*Total*
Low	47	19	20	86
	(68.1)	(30.6)	(29.1)	43
Medium	14	54.8	21.7	31.5
	(20.3)	(54.8)	()21.7)	31.5
High	8	9	34	51
	(11.6)	(14.5)	(49.3)	25.5
Total	**63**	**62**	**69**	**200**
	(100.0)	**(100.0)**	**(100.0)**	**(100.0)**

The figures given in parenthesis indicate percentages.
χ^2 = 54.49; *df* = 6; Significant at .01 level.

Instruction

Parents impart instruction to children about various issues of day-to-day life. The views of parents in this aspect was compared to test the hypothesis that there is no significant difference between fathers and mothers in their extent of use of mechanism of imparting instruction to children. The result is depicted in Table 4.3.6.

Table 4.3.6. 3 × 3 Contingency Table: Comparison of Instruction by Fathers and Mothers

Mother's Instruction	*Fathers' Instruction*			
	Low	*Medium*	*High*	*Total*
Low	42	25	7	75
	(61.6)	(36.1)	(11.3)	37.5
Medium	15	47.8	41.9	75
	(22.7)	(47.2)	(49.9)	37.5

High	9	12	29	50
	(13.6)	(16.7)	(36.8)	25
Total	**66**	**72**	**62**	**200**
	(100.0)	**(100.0)**	**(100.0)**	**(100.0)**

The figures given in parenthesis indicate percentages.
$\chi^2 = 46.56$; $df = 4$; Significant at .01 level.

Perusal of the above table unveils that the perception of fathers and mothers regarding instruction differed significantly leading to the rejection of hypothesis which states that there is no significant difference between fathers and mothers with respect to the imparting instruction.

Investment of Time, Interest and Resources

Parents engage in activities of education of children like attending P.T.A, attending special events in school, going on outing with family etc. In this regard, an attempt was made to compare the investment of time, interest and resources by fathers and mothers. The result is insignificant as reflected in Table. 4.3.7.

Table 4.3.7. 3x3 Contingency Table: Comparison of Investment of Time, Interest and Resources by Fathers and Mothers

Mother's Investment	*Fathers' Investment of time, Interest, Resources*			
	Low	*Medium*	*High*	*Total*
Low	38	25	11	72
	(56.3)	(31.3)	(19.6)	36.0
Medium	18.0	37.0	14.0	69.0
	(28.1)	(46.3)	(25.0)	34.5
High	10.0	18.0	31.0	59.0
	(15.6)	(22.5)	(25.0)	34.5
Total	64.0	80.0	56.0	200.0
	(100.0)	(100.0)	(100.0)	(100.0)

The figures given in parenthesis indicate percentages.
$\chi^2 = 35.57$; $df = 4$ significant at .01 level.

Since the value of Chi-Square is 35.57, the hypothesis H_0 3.5 that there is no significant difference between fathers and mothers in their investment of time, interest and resources is rejected. This means that the ways in which fathers invested their time, interest and resources were much different from that of mothers. The difference in scores is not due to chance.

It is clear that parents engage themselves in various academic activities of children which have a positive influence. At the same time, their perception regarding such activities differ significantly, evident from the Chi-Square values obtained for each component of parental involvement. The above comparison confirm that both the parents differing with respect to the process of involvement in children's education.

Discussion

To summarise, the section in research on the processes of parental involvement, it can be seen that the impact of parental involvement arises from parents' beliefs about them for being involved in the education of children due to motivational factors like Self-efficacy and role construction. The mean scores for the two dimensions of parental involvement were higher than corresponding neutral scores indicating high level of motivation for becoming involved in the education of children.

The results are in consonance with that of Hoover-Dempsey and Sandler (1995). Their theory suggested that parental role construction is a significant contributor to parents' decisions about becoming involved in children's education, because it establishes, at a personal level, the range of activities that parents are likely to construe as important, necessary, and permissible for their own actions with and on behalf of children's education. Composed of values, goals and expectations, as well as characteristic patterns of thinking about the responsibilities and behaviour associated with parental engagement in children's schooling, role construction contributes to parents' schooling. Combined with parents' sense of efficacy for helping the child succeed in school (a personal assessment of how effective one might expect to be, if involved) parental role construction is believed to exert significant influence over parents' basic decisions about active engagement in children's education.

Parental involvement is exhibited continuously through the use of mechanisms of involvement in the form of exhibiting modelling behaviour, providing encouragement, reinforcement, instructions and also by their investment of time, interest and resources. In this study, their involvement activities with reference to day-to-day issues, suggest parents generally exhibit modelling behaviour. They appeared to focus good deal of routine, education-related thinking about the child on ways of encouraging child, giving appropriate instruction and reinforcing their positive behaviours.

The finding reveal that the scale of the impact of parental involvement is evident across all types of schools. There are however, important differences in how parents model value and support the academic activities of their wards. Some of the dimensions of these differences are associated with the parent's values or feelings of self-confidence or efficacy. Some parents do not see it as the part of their 'role' to be a partner in education in their children. Others would like to participate but do not know how to provide encouragement and reinforcement. Variations are due to the way of imparting instruction. Yet, others do not get involved due to lack of time or resources. The way in which fathers set example for their children varied from school to school. Perception of fathers differed significantly with regard to appreciation and providing positive reinforcement to children. Fathers' way of imparting instruction towards regarding how to plan their work, do home work, and have an attitude towards studies etc. were not similar. They differed with respect to the magnitude of imparting instruction.

Comparison of the perceived parental involvement by fathers reveals the diversity in perception with specific reference to type of schools. Self-efficacy is comparatively low among fathers of Government school students and maximum in private schools. Similarly, percentage of parents in private school who provide modeling behaviour far exceeded than those of Government schools.

In the mechanisms of parental involvement, namely encouragement, modeling behaviour reinforcement and instructions, difference could be observed. Encouragement provided by fathers is high in private and central schools and comparatively low in government schools. On the contrary with respect to reinforcement, it is low with fathers of private schools and more in government schools.

Mechanism of instruction is given maximum by fathers of central school students and minimum by fathers of government aided schools.

With respect to investment of time interest and resources, the difference is significant. The percentage is high with fathers of private school students and comparatively low in the case of fathers of Aided school students.

Regarding mothers' perception, the trend is more or less similar. Self-efficacy beliefs of mothers of government school students is low when compared to those of central schools. But difference is insignificant with respect to role construction, mechanism of encouragement and reinforcement.

However, the modelling behaviour as perceived by mothers of central school students is higher than that of mothers of government school students With regards to instruction the difference is significant with low percentage in government schools and high in private schools.

Interestingly, the difference is significant in the dimension - Investment of time resources and interest with comparatively low percentage in private schools and high in government schools.

Thus, the analysis of mothers' perception regarding their involvement in education of children revealed that there was significant difference in the way in which mothers set examples for children. The perception regarding imparting instruction also differ significantly.

It is clear that parents engage themselves in various academic activities of their children which have a positive influence. At the same time, their perception regarding such activities differ significantly. Hence, it can be argued that parents do perceive them as being involved in the academic activities of children, but there is variation in perception regarding motivational factors and the mechanism of involvement due to the type of schools, where their wards studied.

The type of schools where their children studied does matter.

5

Summary, Conclusion and Suggestions

"Parental involvement represents the interdependent lives of young people and their parents. Both may fluctuate with time and changing conditions and both are best viewed as trajectories."

— *(Crosnoe 2001, p. 213)*

The linkage between family and adolescent academic experiences is part of a dynamic process unfolding over time. Parental involvement is a multidimensional construct which has been closely analysed by educationists concerned with the academic development of children. Over the past two decades, growing evidence has shown that parents are valuable resources for public education, one that remains largely untapped with optional outcome for students.

There have been diverse approaches adopted by social scientists to understand the nature of parental involvement and its impact on children. It is difficult to integrate them into one overarching perspective or decide on the most satisfactory. In this study, parental involvement has been studied with respect to motivational aspects for becoming involved in the education of children, namely their self-efficacy and role construction: and also the uses of mechanism of involvement like encouragement, modelling behaviour, reinforcement and instruction.

Need for the Study

While most practitioners and researchers support the policy direction of increased parent involvement, few agree about what constitutes effective involvement. Confusion persists regarding the activities, goals and desired outcome of various parent involvement programmers and policies. Least is known about parent involvement than what is commonly assumed. Hence, the need to look at the attitudinal components of parental involvement rather than at the participatory activities like attending P.T.A, helping in homework, reading with children, volunteering for school activities, etc., Moreover, empirical evidence indicates that demographic characteristics (gender, educational level, socio-economic status) could facilitate or hinder involvement, but they are not the only ones. Beliefs and attitudes could also play either role.

Prior research sheds light on the relationship between parental involvement and proximal outcome for children. However, research on the contribution of parental involvement is limited in several ways. With only a few exceptions, quantitative research typically operationalises parental involvement using a narrow set of indicators that focus on quantity rather than quality of different types of involvement. A multidimensional representation of parental involvement on the other hand would include motivational and mechanism aspect of parental involvement.

Extensive research linking parent involvement to a variety of positive student outcome has been conducted at virtually all grade levels; educators' understanding of link has been significantly shaped by the predominance of studies at the elementary level. Although, much has been written about the individual variables that affect educational outcome and of the relation, search of literature and analytical studies reveal little has been done to analyse overtime statistical data with focus on high school student.

Relative scarcity of literature on parenting in relevance to adolescents has made the need for such research beneficial for educationists, schools, parents, counselors, policy makers, and adolescents. The study will aid educationists and guidance counsellors understand the background variables shaping academic activities.

In the light of the above need and significance, the investigator took up the following problem:

5.1 Statement of Problem

A Study of Parental Involvement in Senior Secondary Students: Does School Matter?

5.2 Objectives of the Study

The study was carried out keeping in view of the following objectives:

1. To study the motivational factors: for parents to be involved in the education of children.
2. To study the extent of the use of mechanism through which parental involvement influence children's educational outcome.
3. To study the investment of time, interest and resources by parents for being involved in the education of children.
4. To make school-wise comparison of fathers with respect to the motivational factors to be involved in the education of children.
5. To make school-wise comparison of fathers with respect to the use of mechanism through which parental involvement influence children's educational outcome.
6. To make school-wise comparison of fathers with respect to the investment of time, interest and resources for being involved in the education of children.
7. To make school-wise comparison of mothers with respect to the motivational factors to be involved in the education of children.

8. To make school-wise comparison of mothers with respect to the use of mechanism through which parental involvement influence children's educational outcome.
9. To make school-wise comparison of mothers with respect to the investment of time, interest and resources for being involved in the education of children.
10. To find whether fathers differ from mothers with respect to involvement in the education of children.

5.3. Hypotheses of Study

Based on the objectives, following hypotheses were formulated and verified:

H_0 1.1. There is no significant difference in the extent of belief of fathers of children studying in Private, Aided Central and Government schools about their Self-efficacy for being involved in the education of children.

H_0 1.2. There is no significant difference in the extent of belief of fathers of children studying in Private, Aided, Central and Government schools about their roles and responsibilities for being involved in the education of children.

H_0 1.3. There is no significant difference in the extent of belief of fathers of children studying in Private, Aided, Central and Government schools about the mechanism of encouragement in the education of children.

H_0 1.4. There is no significant difference in the extent of belief of fathers of children studying in Private, Aided, Central and Government schools about the mechanism of modeling behaviours in the education of children.

H_0 1.5. There is no significant difference in the extent of belief of fathers of children studying in Private Aided, Central and Government schools about the reinforcement of education of children.

H_0 1.6. There is no significant difference in the extent of belief of fathers of children studying in Private Aided, Central and

Government schools about the instruction in the education of children.

H_0 1.7. There is no significant difference in the extent of belief of fathers of children studying in Private Aided, Central and Government schools about investing time, resources and interest in the education of children.

H_0 2.1. There is no significant difference in the extent of belief of mothers of children studying in Private, Aided Central and Government schools about their Self-efficacy for being involved in the education of children.

H_0 2.2. There is no significant difference in the extent of belief of mothers of children studying in Private Aided, Central and Government schools about the roles and responsibilities for being involved in the education of children.

H_0 2.3. There is no significant difference in the extent of belief of mothers of children studying in Private Aided, Central and Government schools about the encouragement, modeling behaviour, reinforcement and instruction in the education of children.

H_0 2.4. There is no significant difference in the extent of belief of mothers of children studying in Private, Aided, Central and Government schools about the use of mechanism of modelling behaviours of children.

H_0 2.5. There is no significant difference in the extent of belief of mothers of children studying in Private, Aided, Central and Government schools about the use of mechanism of reinforcement of children.

H_0 2.6. There is no significant difference in the extent of belief of mothers of children studying in Private Aided, Central and Government schools about the use of mechanism of instruction in the education of children.

H_0 2..7. There is no significant difference in the extent of belief of mothers of children studying in Private Aided, Central and

Government schools about investing time, resources and interest in the education of children.

H_0 3.1. There is no significant difference between fathers and mothers with respect to their extent of belief of Self-efficacy for involvement in the education of children.

H_0 3.2. There is no significant difference between fathers and mothers with respect to their extent of belief of role construction for involvement in the education of children.

H_0 3.3. There is no significant difference between fathers and mothers with respect to the extent of use of mechanism of encouragement in the education of children.

H_0 3.4. There is no significant difference between fathers and mothers with respect to their extent of use of mechanism of modeling behaviour in the education of children.

H_0 3.5. There is no significant difference between fathers and mothers with respect to their extent of use of mechanism of reinforcement in the education of children.

H_0 3.6. There is no significant difference between fathers and mothers with respect to their extent of use of mechanism of instructions in the education of children.

H_0 3.7. There is no significant difference between fathers and mothers with respect to their investment of time, interest and resources in the education of children.

5.4.1 Population and Sample Groups

The population of the present study comprised parents of senior secondary students studying in various schools of Delhi.

The sample of the study comprised:

I. *Students:* 200 pupils studying in Class XI in Private, Government, Central Government and Government Aided schools of Delhi.

II. *Parents:* 200 fathers and 200 mothers of respective students.

5.4.2. Tools Used

Questionnaire for parents: It was based on Parent Involvement Project (PIP). Parent and Teacher Questionnaire developed by Kathleen V, Hoover- Dempsy, Howard M. Sandler and Joan M.I. Walker and prepared by Darlane Whetsel. The tool for Parents comprised 88 items from seven scales namely Self-efficacy, Role Construction, Encouragement, Modeling, Reinforcement, Instructions and Investment of time, interest and resources. The tools administered to corresponding fathers and mothers were identical and their responses were scored.

5.4.3 Data Collection

The data collected from respective parents were contacted at P.T.I sessions and also through home visits.

5.4.4 Analysis and Interpretation

The data was analysed using various quantitative measures such as measure of Central Tendency, measure of Deviation, and Chi-Square.

For the analysis of questionnaire for students, scoring of responses was done by assigning numerical 5,4,3,2,1 to positive statements and 1,2,3,4,5 to the negative statements. The maximum possible score for each item could be five and minimum score one. Mean for each dimension was calculated from statements under respective dimension and the total means score as well as Standard Deviation.

To compare the perceptions of fathers and mothers regarding their involvement, it was felt that Chi-Square would be the suitable statistical method since the data could be classified into 'mutually exclusive categories. Chi-Square was used for drawing some comparison with respect to type of school.

5.5. Delimitations of Study

- The study was confined only to parents of students studying in the National Capital Delhi.

- Only certain components of parental involvement were studied.
- The study was confined to the process and/mechanism of parental involvement.

5.6. Major Findings of the Study

The major finding of study are given under the following heads:

- *Finding related to motivational aspects and mechanism of involvement by parents.*

With regard to Self-efficacy beliefs, the mean score in this dimension for fathers was 58.62 and that of mothers was 62.50. The mean scores were above the minimum 18 and the neutral 45 showing fathers as well as mothers had high self-efficacy belief. Both the parents perceived themselves to be confident about helping wards, they knew how to supervise child's work and were confident of seeking cooperation from school regarding ward's academic progress.

Parents' construction of roles and responsibilities is an important factor for them to become involved in the education of children. The mean score in this dimension of role construction for fathers was 30.23 and that of mothers was 29.94. Though it was only marginally above the neutral 24, projecting that fathers and mothers were aware of their roles as parents and their responsibilities towards children's education.

With reference to encouragement, scores obtained were higher than the neutral score (42) with mothers' score (55.31) comparatively higher than that of fathers (52.32).

The high scores regarding modeling behaviour by parents (33.90 and 33.49) for fathers and mothers respectively, were above the neutral score of 27, which makes it evident that parents were aware of the need to set examples for children and show their wards how to solve problems, figure things out and also how to learn.

About the extent of reinforcement by parents, mean score in the dimension for fathers was 47.81 and that of mothers was 46.50. The high scores for fathers as well as mothers with reference to the neutral score in this dimension (39) imply that parents perceived them as providing positive reinforcement to children's education with fathers' score slightly more than that of corresponding mothers.

The scores in the dimension of instruction confirmed parents provide valuable instruction to wards. The mean score for fathers was 56.52 and that of mothers was 55.54, much above the neutral score of 45.

In the case of parents' investment of time, interest and resources, the score for fathers (36.97) and mothers (37.10) was above the minimum value of 10 and slightly above the neutral value of 30 which reflect fathers and mothers investing their time to attend PTA, special events in school, go on outing with the family and discuss with children about career opportunities. They were ready to invest resources to a limited extent.

Since the overall score obtained for the dimensions of involvement by fathers (321.33) and mothers (320.38) were higher than the neutral score of 264, it may be inferred that fathers as well as mothers of senior secondary school children had confidence in their abilities to deal with children's activities, aware of their roles and responsibilities, were willing to set examples for children and agreed that they provide encouragement, positively reinforcement valuable instruction and also engage themselves in such involvement activities.

Self-efficacy of fathers of children studying in Private, Aided, Central and Government schools did not vary, $\chi^2 = 7.70$). All fathers irrespective of schools where their children studied to have perceived to have self-efficacy in rearing and caring of children.

Chi-Square value of 3.59 is insignificant fathers' role construction leading to the conclusion that perception of role construction by fathers was not different with respect to type of schools.

The extent of use of encouragement by fathers of children studying in Private, Aided, Central and Government schools about developing confidence, valuing traditions, to be open to new ideas etc. did not differ as indicated by the Chi-Square value ($\chi^2 = 3.18$).

On the other hand, the value of Chi-Square ($\chi^2 = 21.38$) is significant with reference to modeling behaviour. It implies that fathers of children studying in Private, Aided, Central and Government schools differ with respect to their use of mechanism of modelling behaviour, setting as examples for children.

Fathers differed significantly ($\chi^2 = 21.39$) with regards to the extent of use of appreciation and positive reinforcement to their children. The extent of imparting instruction to wards by fathers whose children study in different type of schools regarding how to planning their work, do home work, about positive attitude towards studies were not similar.

A comparison of the investment of Time, Interest and Resources revealed that it varied among fathers of children studying in different type of schools ($\chi^2 = 19.10$).

Irrespective of schools where the children studied, mothers held similar views about their efficacy to involve in the education of children, as the value of Chi-Square was insignificant ($\chi^2 = 3.82$).

Mothers' awareness about duties as parents and the role construction is more or less the same with respect to the type of schools in which the children studied ($\chi^2 = 11.00$).

The mechanism of encouragement by mothers did not vary with respect to the type of school where the children studied ($\chi^2 = 3.82$).

Chi-Square value of 12.40 is significant with reference to modeling behaviour implying that mothers' extent of use mechanism of parental involvement varied with respect to the type of schools where their children were studied.

About to the mechanism of instruction by mothers, significant difference was found— ($\chi^2 = 11.00$). The way of imparting such instruction differed significantly depending on the type of schools where their children studied.

Insignificant Chi-Square value ($\chi^2 = 12.05$) implied the extent of use of mechanism of reinforcement was more or less similar among mothers.

A comparison of mothers' investment of time, interest and resources lead to the conclusion that there is no significant difference in this dimension ($\chi^2 = 11.0$).

Parents engage in variou. academic activities of children which have positive influence. At the same time, their perception regarding such activities differ significantly evident from the Chi-Square values obtained for each component of parental involvement.

5. 8. Implications of Study

Several important implications can be argued, reflecting the outcome.

For Scholars

The present study has viewed parental involvement as the expressed attitude of the parents towards child's academic activities. In this study, parental involvement is measured via perceived Self-efficacy, role construction, modelling behaviour encouragement, teaching and investment of time, interest and resources. Based on this study's finding scholars should view parental involvement in more concrete form of active participation versus the traditional expressed quantitative set of indicators.

Most scholars view parental involvement as the collective participation of both the student's mother and father in educational matters, disregarding potential differential impact of involvement by the student's father and mother independently. Based on the outcome, scholars should acknowledge the difference in perception of parental involvement.

For Counsellors

The research review demonstrates the strong influence how parenting behaviour has on high school students. The finding suggest that counsellors and educators should:

- shift the focus from individual to family system,
- develop new and richer view of parent involvement in academic activities,
- help families becoming more proactive,
- convince parents about the important role in academic activities of children.

Parents of these students may not be familiar, knowledgeable about the functioning of educational system. Providing information and guiding them is crucial.

For Policy Makers

Based on the results, policy makers and practitioners ought to consider policies, practices, and programmes encouraging proactive forms of parental involvement opportunities during student's transition through educational pipeline and coincidentally, the student college choice process (e.g., 11-12th class) like:

- extending time for PTA, conferences,
- developing confidence in their abilities to help wards,
- making them aware of roles and responsibilities,
- providing positive reinforcement,
- giving useful instruction,
- engaging in discussions regarding educational matters.

Most specifically, this study's finding imply that policies and programming efforts ought to focus on educating parents, about the importance of effectively engaging in appropriate discourse with adolescents.

Despite explicit policy compact and research finding, some educational agencies and practitioners continue to either completely neglect or fail to appropriately engage parents consistently throughout the educational pipeline.

Based on this study's finding, pre-college programming efforts should employ strategies aiming to involve parents through educational pipeline, with specific focus on encouraging high frequency of parent-student discourse related to things studied in class, course selection and school activities.

Developing collaborative programs with innovative strategies engaging students, parents, and community require youth educators to become effective in managing collaborative partnership that could help change stakeholders perception of their role in adolescent education.

For Parents

Parents can make significant contribution to their child's education in a number of ways. As teachers, they can provide instruction on how to plan work, how to have good attitude, and how to access information about things that interest him/her. As supporters, they could contribute knowledge and skills, encourage children accessible to new and different experiences or provide additional resources. As role models, they can set examples for children how to learn new things, how to be persistent in efforts or how to solve problems etc.

At primary age, there are a number of home learning support programmes which have shown successful outcome, particularly those promoting positive adjustment and improved literacy. The situation at high school may be different, rather than actual involvement in the educational process. The parental role is more about providing enabling, stimulating and enriching physical and psychosocial environment to the child. This can be achieved if parents become role models for children, reinforcing positive behaviour, providing appropriate instruction in solving problems, and spending sufficient time, interest and resource in the educational activities of children. Having a sense of self-efficacy and being aware of the roles as parents is vital for them being involved.

For Children

Since parental involvement projects the likelihood of students engage in positive academic activities, they should hold frequent discussion with parents.

For Schools

Parents play a vital role in the development and education of children and on the overall success of schools. Parental involvement is a common vehicle for bringing teachers and parents together. Parent involvement programs tend to be directed by the school and attempt to involve them in school activities and or teach parents specific skills and strategies for teaching and reinforcing tasks at home. The emphasis is upon harnessing what parents can do to help the school realise on outcome.

Consequently, schools need to place parental engagement at the centre rather than the periphery of they do. Parental engagement in children's learning makes a difference—it is the most powerful school improvement lever that we have. Parental engagement will not happen in a school without concerted effort, time and commitment of parents and schools. The literature and research evidence shows that the impact of parental engagement on students 'academic activities is significant.

Schools should welcome parents and acknowledge the active involvement contribute significantly to their achievement. Schools should:

- encourage family-school partnership programme,
- develop a repertoire of strategies designed to increase parent involvement at school and at home,
- encourage reluctant parents be involved,
- establish open and two-way lines of communication,
- create productive learning environment,
- harness the resources of parents as educationists.

5.9 Suggestions for Further Research

Based on the findings parental involvement during high school years, future research in these areas is warranted.

Such studies should examine the effects of proactive forms of parental involvement such as frequent participation in school activities, helping in studies etc.

In a similar vein, further research could address the effectiveness of various types of parental involvement programmes and opportunities (school governance, parent advisory committees, classroom volunteering, effective parental guidance classes, PTA's, school, family and community outreach programmes) engage students, school staff, and parents debating on school and student matters. Once successful programming efforts are identified, assessment of these programmes could be conducted to identify best practices, which could be emulated by other schools.

The question remains whether students whose fathers are more frequently involved in educational matters have significantly higher educational outcome when compared to their mothers', future research examining time-varying differences on the impact of maternal and paternal involvement could be taken up.

The findings of this study, therefore highlights the need to encourage parental involvement. It is crucial to improve the existing parental involvement projects in our country with the aim of sensitising parents, students and school with contemporary and accurate notion of what is parental involvement and what is its significance.

The findings of the study present at least one consideration scholars should take into account when conducting future studies. The present study has focussed primarily on parents of senior secondary students and has not explicitly explored the parents of students pursuing courses in the institutions of higher education.

The significance of this study was to uncover the relevance of parental involvement with the high school students. It was difficult to develop a complete study because it was limited to only few schools. Further studies should include parental involvement in a variety of schools with different socio-economic backgrounds, races, and levels of administration involvement.

"It's time to start thinking about parents as tools for learning."

Bibliography

Adams, G. (1994). *The family-school connection: Theory, research and practice.* Thousand Oaks, CA: SAGE, pp. 108-54.

Adri Menheere and Edith H. Hooge, E.H. (2008). Op de grenzen van het onderwijs. Professioneel onderwijs in de grote stad. Openbare Les. [On the borders of education. Professional urban education. Public lecture.] Hoge school van Amsterdam. Amsterdam: Amsterdam University Press.

Agarwal, B. (1997). *A comparative study of parental encouragement among students of different educational groups of urban and rural adolescents.* Experiments in Education Vol. XXV, (II), 204-07.

Aggarwal, R. and Kapoor, M. (1998). *Parents' participation in children's academic activities in relation to their academic achievement at the primary level.* Journal of Indian Education, pp. 61-67.

Ainley, J. Foreman J. and Sherit, M. (1991). *High School Factors that Influence Students to Remain in School,* Journal of Educational Research (85).

Alston, S. (2002). *Memories of future foretold: A personal look at early intervention: How some succeeded and others faltered on the road to a better life.* College Board Review, 196, pp. 36-41.

Altman, J.H. (1997). *Career Development in the Context of family experiences. In diversity and women's career development: from adolescence to adulthood,* edited by Helen S. Farmer, pp. 229-42. Thousand Oaks, CA: SAGE.

Amato, P. (1987), *Family Processes and the Competence of Adolescents and Primary School Children.* Journal of Youth and Adolescence (18).

Amin, N. (2003). *Participation of Muslim families in the education of girl child.* Abhijeet Publications New Delhi.

Anderson, H. (1999). *Collaborative learning communities* in E. Camell and C. Lodge. (Eds.). Supporting effective Learning. Paul Chapman publishing, 2000.

Asakawa, K. (2001). *Family socialisation practices and their effects on the internalisation of educational values for Asian and white American adolescents.* Applied Developmental Science, 5, 184-94.

Baker, A.J.L. (1997). *Improving parent involvement programs and practice: A qualitative study of parent perceptions.* School Community Journal, 7 (1), pp.126-53.

Balli, S.J., Demo, D.H., and Wedman, J.F. (1998). *Family involvement with children's homework: An intervention in the middle grades.* Family Relations, 47, pp. 149-57.

Bandura, A., Barbaranelli, C., Caprara, G.V., and Pastorelli, C. (2001). *Self-efficacy beliefs as shapers of children's aspirations and career trajectories.* Child Development, 72, pp. 187-206.

Bandura, A. (1977). *Self-efficacy: Toward a unifying theory of behaviour change.* Psychological Review, 84, pp. 191-215.

Bandura, A. (1986). *Social foundations of thought and action: A social cognitive theory.* Englewood Cliffs, NJ: Prentice Hall.

Barber, B.K., and Olsen, J.A. (2004). *Assessing the transition to middle and high school.* Journal of Adolescent Research, 19, pp. 3-30.

Baumrind, D. (1989), *The influence of parenting style on adolescent competence and substance abuse,* Journal of Early Adolescence, 11(1), pp. 56-95.

Becker, H.J. (1997). *Improving parent involvement programs and practice: A qualitative study of parent perceptions.* School Community Journal, 7 (1), pp. 126-153.

Bender, S. (2004). *Factors influencing traditional or non-traditional career related aspirations among female high school students enrolled in science courses.* Thesis report. SSTA Research centre report 94-104.

Birch, L., and Tanja, M. (1998). *Parent's activity related parenting practices predict girls physical activity.* In (Silver spring) 2009 Nov. 17 (11), pp. 2067-74, PMID 19424165.

Bleeker, M.M., and Jacobs, J.E. (2004). *Achievement in math and science: Do mothers' beliefs matter 12 years later?* Journal of Educational Psychology, 96, pp. 97-109.

Bourdieu, P. (1983) The forms of capital. In J. Richardson (Ed.), of theory and research in the sociology of education (pp. 241-258). Westport, CT: Greenwood Bourdieu, P. (1983) The forms of capital. J. Richardson (Ed.), Handbook of theory and research in the sociology of education (pp. 241-58). Westport, CT: Greenwood.

Bourdieu, P. (1998). *Practical Reason: On the Theory of Action.* Cambridge, UK: Polity Press.

Bromfenbrenner, U. (1979). *The ecology of human development.* Cambridge MA: Harvard University press.

Bronstein, P., Ginsburg, G.S., and Herrera, I.S. (2005). *Parental predictors of motivational orientation in early adolescence: A longitudinal study.* Journal of Youth and Adolescence, 34, pp. 559-75.

Bruner. J. (1999). *Developing Theories of Intention Social Understanding and Self-Control.* Edited by Philip David Zelazo Janet Wilde Astington David R. Olson University of Toronto Lawrence Erlbaum Associates, Publishers Mahwah, NJ. London.

Buhler, C. (1937). *From birth to maturity in Outline of the psychological development of the child.* London: Kegan-Paul.

Byrant, K., Zvonkovic. M., Reynolds, P. (2006) *Parenting in relation to child and adolescent vocational development,* Journal of vocational behaviour August, pp. 149-71.

Cabrera, A.F. and LaNasa, S.M. (2000). *Overcoming the tasks on the path to college for America's disadvantaged.* In A. Cabrera and S. LaNasa (Eds.) Understanding the college choice of disadvantaged students: Vol. 107. New directions for institutional research, pp. 31-44. San Francisco: Jossey-Bass.

Campbell, j., and Mandel (1990). *Connecting Math Achievement to Parental Influences, Contemporary Educational Psychology* (15).

Camhell, L. (1992). Parents and schools working for student success NASSP Bulletin, 76 (543), pp. 10-14.

Carillo, L.W. (1957). *Development of factors to reading ability in children.* Third Review of educational Research -29, 54-64.

Catsambis, S. (1998). *Expanding knowledge of parental involvement in secondary education: Social determinants and effects on high school academic success* (Report 27). Baltimore: Johns Hopkins University, Center for Research on the Education of Students Placed at Risk.

Chavkin, N.F., and Williams, D.L (1987). *Enhancing Parent Involvement. Education and Urban Society* 19, pp. 164-84.

Christenson, S.L. and Godber, Y. (2001). Enhancing constructive family school connections. Handbook of psychological services for children and adolescents, pp. 455-76.

Clayton, K. (1992). *The Role of Family in the Educational and Occupational Decisions Made by Mexican-American Students.* Berkeley, CA: National Center for Research in Vocational Education, (ED357270).

Cohn, M. (1981) *Observations of learning to read and write naturally.* Language Arts, 58, pp. 549-55.

Cokley, K. Komarraju, M., King, A., Cunningham, D., and Muhammad, G. (2003). *Ethnic differences in the measurement of academic self-concept in a sample of African American and European American college students.* Educational and Psychological Measurement, 63, pp. 707-22.

Coleman, J.S. (1991). *Parental Involvement in Education.* Washington, DC: U.S. Department of Education.

Collins, C.H., Moles, O.C., and Cross, M. (1982). *The Home School Connection: Selected Partnership Programmes in Large Cities.* Boston, MA: Institute for Responsive Education.

Collins, W.A., and Laursen, B. (2004). *Parent-adolescent relationships and influences.* In R.M. Lerner and L. Steinberg (Eds.), Handbook of Adolescent Psychology (2nd ed., pp. 331-62). Hoboken, NJ: Wiley.

Comer, J.P. (1988) Is *'Parenting' Essential to Good Teaching?* NEA Today 6: pp. 34-40.

Conners, L.J., and Epstein, J.L. (1995). *Parents and school partnerships.* In M.H. Bornstein (Ed.), Handbook of Parenting (Vol. 4, pp. 437-58). Hillsdale, NJ: Erlbaum.

Cooper, C.R., Grotevant., H.D. Moore, M.S. and Condon, S.M (1982). *Family and conflict. Both foster adolescent identity and role taking.* Paper presented at the meeting of American Psychological Association Washington. D.C.

Cotton, K., and Wikelund, K.R. (2001). *Parent involvement in education,* retrieved October 12, 2004 from Northwest Regional Education Laboratory. Web site.(http)www.nwrel,org

Crites, J.O. (1978). Career Maturity Inventory, Monterey, CA, CTS/McGraw-Hill.

Cronbach, L.J., and Furby, L. (1970). *How should we measure change — or should we?* Psychological Bulletin, 74, pp. 68-80.

Crosnoe, R. (2001). *Academic orientation and parental involvement during high school.* Sociology of Education, 74, pp. 10-230.

Crozier, G. (1998). *Parents and schools: partnerships or surveillance?* The Journal of Education Policy, 13 (1), pp. 125-36. Cotton.

Darling, N., and Steinberg, L. (1993). *Parenting Style as Context: An Integrative Model.* Psychological Bulletin 113m, pp. 487-96.

Darling, N., and Steinberg, L Dornbuch, S.M. (1994). *Overtime changes in adjustment and competence among authoritative, authoritarian, indulgent and neglectful families.* Child Development, 65, pp. 754-70.

Davies, M., and Kandel, D.B. (1981). *Parental and peer influences on adolescents educational plans: Some further evidence.* American Journal of Sociology, 87(2), pp. 363-87.

Dawson, J.M. (1996). *Parenting style, education specific parenting practice and adolescent's achievement and school result outcomes,* Dissertation abstract. Vol. 57 (January).

DeNeve, K. (1999) *Happy as an extraverted clam? The role of personality for subjective well-being. Current Directions in Psychological Science,* 8(5), 141-44.

DeNys, M., and Wolfe, L.R. (1985). *Learning her place-sex bias in the elementary school classroom.* PEER Report 5. Washington, DC: The

Project on Equal Education Rights of the NOW Legal Defense and Education Fund.

Diener, E., Suh, E.M., Lucas, R.E. and Smith, H.L. (1999) *Subjective well-being: three decades of progress.* Psychological Bulletin, 125(2), pp. 276-302.

Desforges, C., and Abouchaar, A. (2003). *The impact of Parental Involvement, Parental Support and Family Education on Pupil Achievement and Adjustment:* A Review of Literature." DFES Report No. 433, June.

Desimone, L.M. (1999). *Linking parent involvement with student achievement: Do race and income matter?* The Journal of Educational Research, 93(1), pp.11-30.

Dornbusch, S.M., and Ritter, P.L. (1998). *Parents of High School Students: A Neglected Resource.* Educational Horizons 66, pp. 75-77.

Dornbusch, S.M., Reed-Hodgson, Prescott, B.L., and Ritter, P.L. (1992). *The relation of among Asian and Pacific-Americans.* Paper presented at the American Educational Research Association, Washington, D.C. (ERIC Document Reproduction Service No. ED 286 973).

Downey, G. and Coyne, J.C. (1990), *Children of depressed parents: An integrative review, Psychological Bulletin,* Vol. 108, pp. 50-76.

Downs, (1996). *Parenting style, Education specific parenting practices and Adolescent achievement and school outcomes.* Dissertation abstracts in Vol. 57, January 1997.

Drake, D.D (2000). *Parents and families as partners in the education process: Collaboration for the success of students in public schools.* ERS Spectrum 34-35.

Dweek, C.S. (1986). *Motivational processes affecting learning: psychological science and education (Special Issue) American Psychologist,* 41, pp. 1040-1048.

Eccles, J.S., and Harold, R.D. (1983). *Parent School Involvement during the early adolescent years. Teachers College record,* 94, pp. 568-87.

Eccles, J.S. and Wigfield, A. (2002). *Motivational beliefs, values, and goals.* Annual Review of Psychology, 53, pp. 109-32.

Elder, et al. (1985). Quoted by C.A. Flanagan and J.S Eccles in *Changes in parents' work status and Adolescents: Adolescent at school, Child Development,* Vol. 64. p. 248.

Epstein, Joyce L., and Dauber, Susan L. (1991). *School Programs and Teacher Practices of Parent Involvement in Inner-City Elementary and Middle Schools.* Elementary School Journal 91, pp. 289-305.

Epstein, Joyce 1. (1995). *School/Family/Community Partnerships: Caring for the Children We Share.* Phi Delta Kappan 76, pp. 701-12.

Epstein, Joyce l. (2001). *School, Family, and Community Partnerships: Preparing Educators and Improving Schools.* Boulder, CO: West view.

Fan, X., and Chen, M. (2001). *Parental involvement and students' academic achievement: A meta-analysis.* Educational Psychology Review, 13 (1), pp. 1-22.

Farnill (1986). *Perception of parental responsibility for child rearing and children's career development. Australian journal of sex, marriage and family.* Vol. 7, No. 4. pp. 207-16.

Fehrmann, P.G.; Keith, T.Z.; and Reiners, T.M. 1987. *Home Influence on School Learning: Direct and Indirect Effects of Parental Involvement on High School Grades.* Journal of Educational Research 80, pp. 330-36.

Francis, A., (2008). *Effects of early intervention on intellectual and academic achievement, a follow up study of children from low-income families.* Article first published on line 28th Jun 2008. DOL: 10.1111/ 1467-8624.1994.

Freud, Sigmund. (1967). *Encyclopedia of Philosophy,* Vol. 3 (ed. P. Edwards). Collier Macmillan.

Furstenberg, F. and Hughes, M. (1995), *Social Capital and Successful Development among At-Risk Youth, Journal of Marriage and the Family* (57), pp. 580-92.

George, R., and Kaplan, D. (1998). A *structural model of parent and teacher influences on science attitudes of eighth graders*: Evidence from NELS: 88, Science Education, 82, pp. 93-109.

Gibson, J.J. (2007). *Parental influence on youth propensity to join the military*. Journal of vocational behaviour. 525-41.

Gilbert, S. and McRoberts, H. (1977). *Academic Stratification and Educational Plans: A Reassessment*, Canadian Review of Sociology and Anthropology 14(1).

Ginsburg, G., and Bronstein. P. (1993). *Family factors related to children's intrinsic/extrinsic motivational orientation and academic performance child development*, 64, pp. 1461-74.

Gonzalez, A., Greenwood, G.E., and Wen Hsu. J. (2001). *Undergraduate students 'goal Orientations and their relationship to perceived parenting styles*. College Student Journal, 35, pp. 182-92.

Goodson, B.D., and Hess, R.D. (1975). *Parents as Teachers of Young Children: An Evaluative Review of Some Contemporary Concepts and Programs*. Washington, DC: Bureau of Educational Personnel Development, DHEW, May 1975. (ED 136 967).

Gordon, I.J. (1979). *The Effects of Parent Involvement on Schooling. In Partners: Parents and Schools*, edited by R.S. Brandt. Alexandria, VA: Association for Supervision and Curriculum Development, 1979.

Gottfredson, G.D., and Holland, J.L. (1989). *Dictionary of Holland occupational codes* (2nd ed.). Odessa, FL: Psychological Assessment Resources.

Gottfredson, I.S. (1981). *Circumscription and Compromise: A Developmental Theory of Occupational Aspirations*, Journal of Counseling Psychology (28), pp. 545-79.

Grewal, J.S. (1975). *Level of aspiration measure National Psychological Cooperation*, Raja Mandi; Agra.

Griffith, J. (1996). *Relation of parental involvement, empowerment, and schools traits to student academic performance*, The Journal of Educational Research, 91 (1), pp. 33-41.

Grimstad, J.A., and Way, W.L. (1993). *The Role of Family in the Vocational Development of Family and Consumer Education Teachers: Implications for Vocational Education,* Journal of Vocational Education Research 18, No. 4, pp. 43-80.

Grolnick, Wendy S., and Slowiaczek, Maria L. (1994). *Parent's Involvement in Children's Schooling: A Multidimensional Conceptualisation and Motivational Model.* Child Development 65, pp. 237-52.

Hannah, J.S., and Kahn, S.E. (1989). *The relationship of socio-economic status and gender to occupational choices of grade 12 students.* Journal of Vocational Behaviour, 34, pp. 161-78.

Hanushek, E.A., Kain, J.F., Markman, J.M., and Rivkin, S.G. (2003). *Does peer ability affect student achievement?* Journal of Applied Econometrics, 18, pp. 527-44.

Harris, A., and Goodall, J. (2007). *Engaging parents in raising achievement. Do parents know they matter?* London Department for children, Schools and families.

Henderson, A. (1987). *The Evidence Continues to Grow: Parent Involvement Improves Student Achievement-An Annotated Bibliography.* Columbia, MD: National Committee for Citizens in Education, 1987.

Henderson, A. and Berla (1994). *A New Generation of Evidence.* Washington, DC: National Committee for Citizens in education, 1994. pp. 160.

Herr, E.L. (1970). *Decision-making and vocational development.* Boston: Houghton Mifflin.

Hess, R.D, and Holloway, S.D. (1984). *Family and school as educational institutions.* In R.D. Parke (Ed.), Review of child development research: Vol. 7. The family, pp.179-222. Chicago: University of Chicago Press.

Hill, N.E., and Craft, S.A. (2003). *Parent-school involvement and school performance: Mediated pathways among socio-economically comparable African American and Euro-American families.* Journal of Educational Psychology, 95(1), pp. 74-83.

Ho, I.T. (2001). Are Chinese teachers authoritarian? In D.A. Watkins and J.B. Biggs (Eds.), *Teaching the Chinese learner: psychological and pedagogical perspectives*, Hong Kong Comparative Education Research Center, University of Hong Kong, pp. 99-115.

Holland, J.L. (1985). *Making vocational choices: A theory of vocational personalities and work environments.* Englewood Cliffs, N.J.: Prentice-Hall.

Holland, J.L., Gottfredson, G.D., and Baker, H.G. (1990). *Validity of vocational aspirations and interest inventories: Extended, replicated and reinterpreted.* Journal of Counseling Psychology, 37, pp. 337-42.

Hoover Dempsey, Kathleen, V., and Sandler, Howard, M. (1995). *Parent Involvement in Children's Education: Why does it Make a Difference?* Teachers College Record 97, pp. 310-31.

Hoover Dempsey, Kathleen, V., and Sandler, Howard, M. (1997). *Why Do Parents Become Involved in Their Children's Education?* Review of Educational Research 67, pp. 3-42.

Horrocks, J.E. (1951). *Psychology of adolescent behaviour and development*, Houghton, Mifflin, digitised in 2008.

Hossler, D. and Stage, F.K. (1992). *Family and high school experience influence on postsecondary educational plan of 9th grade students.* American Educational Research Journal, 29, pp. 425-51.

Hurlock. Elizabeth. B. (1980). *Development Psychology Life span approach* 5th edition by Tata McGraw Hill Higher Education, First published 1698.

Hurrae, T. (2006). *Health, lifestyle, family and school factors in adolescence: predicting adult educational level.* Educational Research, Vol. 48, No. 1, pp. 41-51.

IIngels, S.K., Scott, L.A., Taylor, J.R., Ownings, J. and Quinn, P. (1998). *National educational Longitudinal study of 1998 (NELS88) base year through second follow up. Final methodology report.* Washington D.C. National center for educational statistics.

Jackson, G.A. (1982). *Public efficiency and private choice in higher education. Educational Evaluation and Policy Analysis,* 4(2), pp. 237-47.

Jane, E.P., Zenobia., and Slatton, L. (2007). *The function of family involvement in adolescents' aspiration and achievement. Issues in the psychology of motivation.* Nova Science Publications, pp. 65-99.

Jeynes, W.H. (2005). *Parental involvement and student achievement: A meta-analysis* (Family Involvement Research Digest). Cambridge, MA: Harvard Family Research Project. Retrieved January 1, 2007, fromh ttp://www.gse.harvard.edu/hfrp/publications_resources/publications_series/family_ involvement_research_digests/parental_ involvement_ and_student_achievement_a_meta analysis.

Jencks, C., and Mayer, S. (1990). *The social consequences of growing up in a poor neighborhood.* In L.E. Lynn and M.F.H. McGeary (Eds.), Inner-city poverty in the United States, pp. 111-86. Washington, DC: National Academy Press.

Jussim, L., Eccles, I. and Madon, S. (1996). *Social perceptions, social stereotypes and teacher expectations. Accuracy and the quest for the powerful self-fulfilling prophecy.* Advances in Experimental Social Psychclogy, 28, pp. 281-388.

Kaiser, (1997). *The effects of parental homework monitoring intervention on school engagement of high risk middle school students. Doctoral dissertation,* University of Oregon, 1997. Dissertation Abstracts International, 58.

Kao, G. and Tienda, M. (1998). *Educational aspirations of minority* youth American Journal of Education, 106, pp. 349-84.

Kaplan, A., Middleton, M.J., Urdan, T. and Midgley, C. (2002). *Achievement goals and goal structures.* In C. Midgley (Ed.) *Goals, goal structures and patterns of adaptive learning Hillsdale,* NJ: Erlbaum, pp. 21-54.

Keith, T.Z. (1986). *Parent Involvement, Homework, and TV Time: Direct and Indirect Effects on Achievement.* Journal of Educational Psychology 78, pp. 373-80.

Kellaghan, T., Sloane, K., Alvarez, B., and Bloom, B.S. (1993). *The Home Environment and School Learning: Promoting Parental Involvement in the Education of Children.* San Francisco: Jossey-Bass.

Kelly, K.R. (1993). *The relation of gender and academic achievement to career self-efficacy and interests.* Gifted Child Quarterly, 37, pp. 59-64.

Kandel, D.B. and Andrews, K. (1987). *Processes of adolescent socialisation by parents and peers.* International Journal of Addictions, 22(4), 319-42.

Kim Witko, Kerry Bbernes, Kris Magnusson, and Angelena, D. Bardik (2005). *Senior high school career planning: what students want.* Journal of educational enquiry, Vol. 6, No. 1.

Kline, R.B. (2005). *Principles and practice of structural equation modeling* (2nd ed.). New York: Guilford Press.

Kohl, G.O., Lengua, L.J., McMahon, R.J., and the Conduct Problems Prevention Research Group. (2000). *Parent involvement in school: Conceptualising multiple dimensions and their relations with family and demographic risk factors.* Journal of School Psychology, 38, pp. 501-38.

Kohn, M.L. (1963). *Social class and parent-child relationships.* American sociological Review, 8, pp. 471-80.

Kothari, C.R. (2004). *Research Methodology: Methods and Techniques.* New age International publishers 2nd edition, New Delhi.

Kracke, B. (1997). *Parental behaviours and adolescents' career exploration.* The Career Development Quarterly, 45, p. 341.

Krumboltz, J.D., Mitchell, A.M., and Jones, B.G. (1978). *A social learning theory of career selection.* In J.M. Whitely and A. Resnikoff (Eds.), Career counseling (pp. 100-127). Monterey, CA: Brooks/Cole.

Kumar, R., and Hruda, L.Z. (2001). *What do I want to be when I grow up? Role of parent and teacher support in enhancing student's academic confidence and educational expectations.* Paper presented at the annual meeting of the American Educational Research Association (AREA) Seattle, Washington.

Kurts and Swenson (1951). *Foundations of Psychological Research.* Boston. Sts and Mc.Mrmt.1965.

Lamborn, S., Mounts, N., Steinberg, L., and Dornbusch, S. (1991). *Patterns of competence and adjustment among adolescents from authoritative,* authoritarian, indulgent, and neglectful families. Child Development, 62(5), pp. 1049-1065. (EJ 436 489).

Lareau, A. (1987). *Social Class Differences in Family-School Relationships: The Importance of Cultural Capital Sociology of Education,* 60 (April), pp. 73-85.

Lent, R.W., Brown, S.D., and Hackett, G. (2000). *Contextual supports and barriers to career choice: A social cognitive analysis.* Journal of Counseling Psychology, 47, pp. 36-49.

Levine, D.V., and Lezott, Z.W. (1995). Effective school research, in Ormrod J.E (Eds) *Educational Psychology Developing learners* Merrillm Prentice-Hall.

Lewin, K. (1956). *Psychology of success and failure.* Occupations, pp. 926-30.

Lidz, T. (1970). The family as the developmental setting In E.J. Anthony and C. Koupernick. (Edu).*The child in his family.* New York. John Wiley and sons, Inc.

Lin, C. and Atkin, D. (1989). *Parental Mediation and Rule making for Adolescent Use of Television and VCRs,* Journal of Broadcasting and Electronic Media (33).

Loyd-Smith, L., and Baron, M. (2010). *Beyond Conferences: Attitudes of High School Administrators Toward Parental Involvement in One Small Midwestern State.* The School Community Journal, 20(2), pp. 23-44.

Ma, X. (2001). *Participation in advanced mathematics: Do expectation and influence of students, peers, teachers, and parents matter?* Contemporary Educational Psychology, 26, pp. 132-46.

Marjoribanks, K. (1996). *Ethnicity, Proximal Family Environment, and Young Adolescents' Cognitive Performance.* Journal of Early Adolescence 16, pp. 340-59.

Marso, R., and Pigge, F. (1994). *Personal and family characteristics associated with reasons given by teacher candidates for becoming teachers in the 1990's: implications for the recruitment of teachers.* Paper presented at the Annual Conference of the Midwestern Educational Research Association, Chicago, IL, October 15, 1994. (ED 379 228).

Martinez-Pons, M. (1996). *Test of a model of parental inducement of academic self- regulation.* Journal of Experimental Education, 64(3), pp. 312-27.

Mattingley, D.J., Prislin, R., McKenzie, T.L., Rodriguez, J.L., and Kayzar, B. (2002) *Evaluating evaluations: the case of parent involvement programmes.* Review of Educational Research, 4, pp. 549-76.

Middleton, E.B., and Loughead, T.A. (1993). *Parental Influence on Career Development: An Integrative Framework for Adolescent Career Counseling,* Journal of Career Development 19, No. 3 (Spring 1993), pp. 161-73.

Miller, S.A., (1988). *Parents belief about Children's Development Child Development,* 59, pp. 259-85.

Moles, O.C. (1982). *Synthesis of Recent Research on Parent Participation in Children's Education.* Educational Leadership 40, pp. 44-47.

Montgomery, J. (1992). *Factors that Influence the Career Aspirations of Mathematically Precocious Females.* Paper presented at the Asian Conference on Giftedness: Growing Up Gifted and Talented, Taipei, Taiwan, (ED352267).

Mortimer, J. Mosychuck and Majoribanks, K. (1992). *Influences on Adolescents' Vocational Development.* Berkeley, CA: National Center for Research in Vocational Education, (ED352555).

Muller, C. (1993). *Parent Involvement in Home, School and Community. In Parents, Their Children and Schools,* eds. Barbara Schneider and James Coleman, 13-42. Boulder, Colo.: West view Press.

Muller, C. (1993). *Parental Involvement and Academic Achievement: An Analysis off family Resources Available to the Child,"* Parents, Their Children and Schools, Boulder, West view.

Neumayer, M.H. (1949). *Juvenile Delinquency in Modern Society.* Newyork: Nostrand pp. 118-23.

OECD (2010), PISA 2009 Results: *Learning to Learn — Student Engagement, Strategies and Practices* (Vol. III) http://dx.doi.org/10.1787/9789264083943-en

Osipow, S.H. (1983). *Theories of career development* (3rd ed.) Englewood Cliffs, NJ: Prentice-Hall.Otto Henry, j. 1956 Social education in Elementary Schools. New York. Rinehart and C.D-1956. Rinehart books in elementary Education.

Otto, L.B. and V.R.A. Call. (1985). *Parental Influence on Young People's Career Development.* Journal of Career Development 12(1) 65-69.

Palmonari, A., Kirchler, E., and Pombeni, M.L. (1991). *Differential effects of identification with family and peers on coping with developmental tasks in adolescence.* European Journal of Social Psychology, 21, pp. 381-402.

Parsons, J.E., Adller, T.F. and Kaczala, C.M (1992). *Socialisation of Achievement, Attitudes and Beliefs.* Parental Influence. Child Development, 53, pp. 310-21.

Perna, L.W. and Titus, M.A. (2005). *The relationship between parental involvement social capital and college enrollment: An examination of racial/ethnic group differences.* Journal of Higher Education, 76(5), pp. 486-518.

Penick, N., and Jepsen, D. (1992). *Family Functioning and Adolescent Career Development.* Career Development Quarterly 40, No. 4 pp. 208-22.

Prakash, J. (1996). *Influence of demographic variables on learners 'achievement. A trend analysis of DPEP states.* Indian Educational Review. Vol. 31 (1) 36-45.

Pringle, D.G. and Walsh, J. (1999). *Poor people, poor places: An introduction.* In D.G. Pringle, J. Walsh and M. Hennessey (Eds.) *Poor people, poor places: A geography of poverty and deprivation in Ireland.* Dublin: Oak Tree Press.

Purohit, S., and Parveen N. (2008). *Role of parenting styles in nurturing the self-concept among adolescents girls,* Edutracks (Feb) Vol. 7 pp. 34-38.

Rainey, L.M., and Borders, L.D. (1997). *Influential factors in career orientation and career aspiration of early adolescent girls.* Journal of Counseling Psychology, 44, pp. 160-72.

Rajput, K.S. (1992). *Educational Aspirations and Academic achievement of Secondary school students.* Indian Educational review Vol. 27, No. 1.

Rao, Q.B. and Rao, K.R. (1996). *Current Trends in Indian Education.* Discovery Publishing House, New Delhi.

Rao, Nalini (1989). *Parent-Child Relationship Scale. National Psychological Cooperation.* Agra, India.

Redding, S. (1999). *Parents and Learning. Brussels: International Academy of Education.*

Reynolds, A.J., and Gill, S. (1994). *The role of parental perspectives in the school adjustment of inner-city Black children.* Journal of Youth and Adolescence, 23, pp. 671-95.

Ritchie, C., Flouri, E. and Buchanan, A. (2005). *Aspirations and Expectations.* Policy Discussion Paper: National Family and Parenting Institute.

Ritter, P.L. Monts, R. and Dornbusch, S.M. (1993). *Minority parents and their youth: concern, encouragement and support for school achievement.* In M.F. Chavkin (Ed) families and school in a pluralistic society 1993, (pp. 107-120). Albany State University of New York.

Roe, A. (1956). *The Psychology of Occupation,* John Wiley and Sons Inc., New York. Cleapan and Hall Limited, London.

Rosen, B.C. (1959). *Family structure and achievement motivation.* American Sociological Review 26: pp. 574-578, Rosen, B.C. (1959). Rosen, B.C. (1973). *Social Change, Migration and Family Interaction in Brazil.* American Sociological Review 38, pp. 198-212.

Russell, C.N., Warrack, B.J., and Bremner, L.K. (1978). *Post-secondary plans, aspirations and profile characteristics of grade twelve students in Manitoba, Manitoba, Winnipeg, Canada: Post Secondary Research Reference Committee.* ERIC Document Reproduction Service No. ED 160 026.

Ryan, B.A., and Adams, G.R. (1985). *The Family-School Partnership Model in The Family-School Relationship Model in The Family School Connection Theory Research and Practice by Bruce,* A.R., London, Sage publications.

Sacker, A., Schoon, I., and Bartley, M. (2002). *Social inequality in educational achievement and psychological adjustment throughout childhood: magnitude and mechanisms.* Social Science and Medicine, 55, pp. 863-80.

Sanders, M.G. and Epstein, J.L. (2000). *The national network of partnership schools: How research influences educational practice,* Journal of education for students placed at risk, 5 (1-2), pp. 61-76.

Schoon, I., and Parsons, S. (2002). *Competence in the face of adversity: the influence of early family environment and long-term consequences,* Children and Society, 16, pp. 260-72.

Schulenberg, J.E., Vondracek, F.W., and Croutter, A.C. (1984). *The influence of the family on vocational development.* Journal of Marriage and the Family, pp. 129-43.

Scott-Jones, D. (1985). *Parent-child interactions and school achievement in the family-school connections Theory Research and Practice by Bruce,* A.R. et al., London SAGE Publications.

Seginer, R. (1983). *Parents' Educational Expectations and children's Academic Achievement: A Literature Review,* Merrill-palmer Quarterly 29, pp. 1-23.

Seidman, E., Allen, L., Aber, J.L., Mitchell, C., and Feinman, J. (1994). *The impact of school transitions in early adolescence on the self-system and perceived social context of poor urban youth.* Child Development, 65, pp. 507-22.

Sharma, J. (1974). *Study of Parental Value Orientations and their Level of Aspiration as Correlates of Academic Achievements of their Children.* Psychological Abstracts, Vol. 8. pp. 3619-21.

Sharma, S. and Nidhi, (2002). *A Study of the effect of Parental Involvement and Aspirations of Achievement of +2 Doctoral Theses.* Punjab University, Chandigarh, India.

Singh, K. Bickley, P.G., Keith, T.Z., Keith, P.B., Trivette, P., and Anderson, E. (1995). *The effects of four components of parental involvement on eighth-grade student achievement: Structural analysis of NELS-88 data.* School Psychology Review, 24, pp. 299-317.

Slaughter, and Defoe, D.J. (1993). *Revisiting the concept of socialisation Care giving and teaching in the 90's. A personal perspective.* American psychologist, 50 (4), pp. 276-36.

Snary. J., (1993). *How fathers care for the next generation. A four decade study.* Cambridge Harvard University press.

Sowers, A. (1937). *Parent-Child Relationship from the Child's Point of View.* Journal of experimental education, pp. 205-31.

Sowell, T. (1984). *Civil Rights: Rhetoric or reality?* New York: William Morrow.

Steinberg, L., (1996). *Beyond the Classroom.* New York: Simon and Schuster.

Straus, A., and Corbin, J. (1990). Basics of qualitative research. Newbury Park, CA: Sage publications. Strage, A.A., and Brandt, T.S. *"Authoritative Parenting and College Students' Academic Adjustment and Success."* Journal of Educational Psychology 91, No. 1 (March 1999): 146-56.

Tang, M. (2003). *Career counseling in the future: constructing, collaborating advocating — career counseling in the next decade,* Career Development Quarterly, Vol. 52, pp. 61-69.

Taris, T. and Bok, I. (1996). *Effects of parenting style upon psychological well-being of young adults: Exploring the relations among parental care, locus of control and depression,* Early child development and care, 132: 93-104.

Tizard, J., Schofield, W.N. and Hewison J. (1982). *Collaboration between Teachers and Parents in assisting Children's Reading British,* Journal of Educational Psychology 52 , pp. 1-15.

Trivedi, V. (1987). *A study of the Relationship of Parental Attitudes background and Feeling of Security among the Intermediate Students and their Academic Achievement.* Ph.D Edu. Lucknow University, India.

Trusty, J. Niles, S.G., and Carney, J.V. (2005). *Education-career planning and middle school counselors.* Professional School Counseling, 9, pp. 136-43.

Van Voorhis, F.L. (2001). *Interactive science homework: An experiment in home and school Connections. National Association of Secondary School Principals Bulletin,* 85(627), pp. 20-32.

Vellamalay, N. (2012) *Bridging School and Parents: Parental Involvement in their Child's Education Journal of Studies in Education* 2012, Vol. 2, No. 1.

Walson, T. Brown, M., and Swick, K.J. *The Relationship of Parents' Support to Children's School Achievement.* (1983) Child Welfare 62: pp. 175-80.

Walker, J.M.T., Wilkins, A.S., Dallaire, J.P., Sandler, H.M., and Hoover-Dempsey, K.V. (in press). *Parental involvement: Model revision through scale development.* Elementary School Journal.

Wardle, J., Robb, K. and Johnson, F. (2002). *Assessing socio-economic status in adolescents: The validity of home affluence scale.* Journal of Epidemiology and Community Health, 56, pp. 595-99.

Way, W.L., and Rossmann, M.M. (1996). *Lessons from life's first teacher: the role of the family in adolescent and adult readiness for school-to-work transition.* Berkeley, CA: National Center for Research in Vocational Education (ED 396 113).

Wigfield, A., and Eccles, J.S. (2006). Development of achievement motivation in N. Eisenberg (Ed.) Handbook of child psychology: Vol. 3. *Social, emotional and personal development,* 6th ed., pp. 933-1002, New York, N.Y: Wiley.

Williams, B., Williams, J., and Ullman, A. (2002). *Parental involvement in Education* (Research Report RR332). Department for Education and Skills.

Wolfendale, and Bastiani, J. (2000). *The contribution of parents to school effectiveness,* (eds.) London: David Fulton Publishers.

Young, R.A. and Friesen, J.D. (1992). *The intentions of parents in influencing the career development of their children.* Career Development Quarterly, 40, 198-207. p.14.

Index